AARONIC
foundational
MINISTRIES

Edited by Paul M. Edwards

Produced in Consultation with
The Presiding Bishopric
and
Temple School Center

Herald Publishing House
Independence, Missouri

Library of Congress Cataloging-in-Publication Data
Aaronic Foundational Ministries / edited by Paul M. Edwards
   p. cm.
   Includes bibliographical references.
   ISBN 0-8309-0718-1
   1. Aaronic Priesthood (RLDS Church) 2. Reorganized Church of
Jesus Christ of Latter Day Saints—Doctrines.   I. Edwards, Paul M.
BX8675.A22 1995
262'.149333—dc20   95-13670
                                                                          CIP

99 98 97 96 95   1 2 3 4 5

Contents

Acknowledgments 9

Foreword by the Presiding Bishopric
    Norman E. Swails 11

I. Aaronic Priesthood

    Chapter 1: The Role of the Aaronic Priesthood
        Paul M. Edwards 15

    Chapter 2: A Brief History of Aaronic
        Quorums. *Mark A. Scherer* . . . 27

    Chapter 3: Survey of Aaronic Educational
        Activities. *Lyman F. Edwards* . . 33

    Chapter 4: Aaronic Ministry and the Temple
        Joni Wilson 37

II. The Aaronic Offices

    Chapter 5: Being a Deacon in Today's
        Church. *Isleta L. Pement* and
        A. Bruce Lindgren 47

    Chapter 6: Teachers for the Twenty-first
        Century. *Ruth Ann Wood* 61

    Chapter 7: Being a Priest in Today's Church
        John W. Noren 77

III. Spirituality

    Chapter 8: Drawn to the Stream:
        Considerations for Personal
        Spirituality. *David D. Schaal* . . 95

    Chapter 9: Spiritual Mentoring and the Lead-
        ings of the Spirit. *John T. Conway*
        and *Charles E. Mader* 127

Chapter 10: Report on the Ministry of Angels
The Presiding Bishopric 155

IV. Outreach and Commitment

Chapter 11: Mission, Vision, and Celebration
Darlene A. Caswell 161

Chapter 12: Stewardship Ministries
Robert L. Logan 169

Chapter 13: Expansion Ministries
Stephen M. Veazey 193

Chapter 14: Communities of JOY
Leonard M. Young 207

Chapter 15: A Concluding Word
Paul M. Edwards 219

Appendix

The Mentor/Ordinand Concept
Leonard M. Young and *John T. Conway* . . . 221

Bibliography

I. Temple School Courses to Aid
Aaronic Skills 229

II. Resources from Herald House 233

III. Adult Texts for Reunion 234

IV. General Resources 236

Acknowledgments

From the early days of the Restoration movement the work of the Aaronic priesthood has, both scripturally and traditionally, been under the general supervision of the Presiding Bishopric. Thus, while the focus of the Aaronic priesthood's responsibility and service is primarily congregational, the quorum has long been guided, and educated, through their association with the Order of Bishops. It is in this responsibility, and in an attitude of prayerful appreciation for the commitment and participation of the Aaronic quorums, that this book was first envisioned.

The development of a collection such as this one involves a great deal of work by many people. The editor would like to acknowledge the significant contribution made by so many.

Special note must be taken of the efforts of the staff of the Temple School Center who focused their considerable talent on this project. Many thanks as well to those who responded to requests for specialized manuscripts including: Darlene A. Caswell, John T. Conway, Lyman F. Edwards, Charles E. Mader, John W. Noren, Isleta L. Pement, David D. Schaal, Mark A. Scherer, Steven M. Veazey, Joni Wilson, Ruth Ann Wood, and Leonard M. Young. To the members of the Presiding Bishopric who envisioned the collection and to the First Presidency who supported it, the editor's grateful thanks.

Foreword

The need for more resource materials in support of the ministries of the Aaronic priesthood has never been greater. We are pleased to introduce this book and recommend it to anyone who has the desire to progress in their personal spiritual journey and has the conviction to give of themselves in the service of others. The topics discussed in the pages that follow are foundational principles that must be in place before corporate spiritual health can be maintained. This is the distinct role of Aaronic ministers as they seek to serve the cause of the kingdom with new eyes, new truths, and new ministries.

It is important to approach the reading and study of these selections with a renewed realization of our personal worth. God has placed within each of us the power and the promise to do many things of our own free will. We do not need to wait for anyone else to empower us. We need not stand by until something outside ourselves changes or until we are specifically asked to minister in a certain way. We have within us the spark of divine nature. To quote an old saying, "We need not fill a vessel, but light a candle."

Realizing that God has provided all—the gifts, skills, and talents within a community of Christ to fulfill the divine purpose—is a beginning point. We sometimes use our lack of "know-how" as an excuse for not taking the first step, finding new methods, or proactively moving forward. But we are called to act. We sincerely hope this resource will enhance the ministry you are already providing in your congregation.

It is our desire that each reader will be enlightened and encouraged by what has been prepared. May the inspiration of the Holy Spirit add its confirming power in the areas of your greatest need and may new avenues of ministry excite you and give you strength and courage is our prayer.

Norman E. Swails
Presiding Bishopric

SECTION I

Aaronic Priesthood

CHAPTER 1

The Role of the Aaronic Priesthood

Religious people are called to the service of their God. For Christians this call is defined by their understanding of Jesus Christ. Within this Christian framework, members of the priesthood have a particular responsibility for service. Perhaps we hear this said so often that we are inclined to take it for granted, thus failing to acknowledge how significant it is. We don't realize just how key service is to members of the Aaronic quorums. For the Aaronic priesthood, this call to service is a unique one that quite often can be taken literally. As "doers" the deacon, the teacher, and the priest are called to a service that is often more directly seen, more easily identifiable. Aaronic ministry is clearly a ministry of relationship, thus a ministry of presence.

The Pillars of Priesthood

While it is important for us to look specifically at the various Aaronic priesthood roles, there is wisdom in stepping back for a brief look at priesthood in more general terms. To begin such a view, first focus on what has often been called the "pillars of priesthood." These pillars focus on the Doctrine and Covenant's affirmation that "All are called according to the gifts of God unto them" (Doctrine and Covenants 119:8b).

The first of these pillars is the full recognition that God is the one who calls us. While the church as a body grants us the authority to act for, and within, the church, it is into God's service that we are called. This call to service is for a specific office and responsibility. While religious people of all persuasions will feel called to respond to the love of God, a call to the priesthood is unique to the person who receives it. This calling emerges out of individual experience and will be fulfilled as ministry out of individual faith experience. But it is, nevertheless, God's call.

The act of accepting priesthood responsibility is, of course, an act of belief. For such a response reaffirms the Restoration concept of God acting in history. In this case, God is acting in the life of a man or a woman who is called to provide specific services: to be the church in the world. Consider this comment from the *Guidelines for Priesthood*.[1]

> Our religious heritage, continued in the church today, affirms the creative acts of God intervening in human history, calling persons and communities into being. From Abraham in Ur of the Chaldees to World Conference ... God has continued to work in the world to effect divine purposes. The form of the call of God to persons changes with the conditions of the world in which those persons live: from the burning bush to the still small voice of inspiration given a local pastor.

The second pillar of our priesthood is that of discipleship. For the response God seeks is one of participation. When Jesus tells us "Feed my sheep" (John 21:16), he is identifying our responsibilities as action, not merely observation. He beckons us to be God's presence. He commissions us and empowers us to love without reservation, to give without hesitation, to live beyond the frustrations of our common lives. In the Doctrine and Covenants 4:1b, c:

...O ye that embark in the service of God, see that ye serve him
with all your heart, might, mind, and strength, that ye may
stand blameless before God at the last day; therefore, if ye have
desires to serve God, ye are called to the work...

Much can be learned by considering the word **disciple,**
which is derived from the same word as **discipline,** and
means "to grasp, to take hold of, to be a teacher in a
possessive manner." Thus when we speak of disciples we
mean learners who are more than followers—followers
who profess. In the biblical accounts of the life of Jesus
Christ, we can identify three kinds of disciples who are
equally as identifiable now as they were 2,000 years ago.

On the one hand are those who come to Christ but, in
effect, do little or nothing more than follow. They like the
atmosphere of the follower; they feel better with the
crowd; they enjoy the association with the celebrity,
however distant that association may be.

A second type of follower is the one who comes not only
to see and be seen but to learn. They come out of curiosity;
they come because they are interested in the ideas; they
like the concepts; and, in general, they are collectors of
ideas and of information. They often see, in the life of
Jesus, an endorsement for their own views. But just as
easily they are not challenged to move beyond that understanding.

A third type of followers are those who represent what
a disciple really should be. These people follow in search
of action. They see in the crowd; they hear from the
lessons; they are motivated by the ideas and the love to
participate in the world of believing and loving. Such a
level of discipleship takes us out of ourselves, removes us
from the limitations of our own parameters, and links us
to the great leader and the great cause that is found in
Jesus Christ.[2]

Yet another pillar to our priesthood is found in our faithful affirmation of our potential. This affirmation arises out of our faith that in making such a call, God identifies that which is deep within us. Despite our obvious limitations, the potential is there; that while we may well represent only a small beginning, we can respond to God's investment in us. We have abilities, talents, commitment, and dedication, and these can all be put into service. Such a faith requires preparation, continued growth, anticipation, and response that allows the power of God to work in us.

None of us enters the responsibilities of priesthood without being aware of his or her limitations. By the same token, we must also be aware of the great possibilities that lie in our commitment. It is in the vision of God's love that we can image the results of our dedication to the work.

The final pillar for consideration is found in the recognition that we are called to be partners with God in the kingdom-building mission of Jesus Christ. This particular partnership requires that we serve as witnesses to the power of God within us. That is, we bear the fruits that are, at their best, the completion of our unique gifts. Not only do these fruits result from what we have been, but they reflect what we can be by virtue of our discipleship. We are the witness to what we have received.

Aaronic Service

The call to Aaronic priesthood is a meaningful call. It can, as well, be a difficult call. For like any really significant service, it carries with it great responsibilities. These responsibilities are to be found in our understanding of, and participation in, the work of the Lord. They are perhaps best understood by looking at the very essence of the Aaronic priesthood member. What is the character of the man or woman who is called to this service? Perhaps we can look at these most easily by listing four fairly arbitrary headings. These illuminate the Aaronic priesthood as vocation, proclaimer, healer, and servant.

The Character of the Aaronic Calling

• ***The Aaronic priesthood as vocation:*** A vocation is a job. A vocation is also often defined as that aspect of your life you consider to be primary. Sometimes this means what you do for a living, or your profession. But for many of us, our primary vocation is our response to the call from God. And, in some very meaningful ways, it is "what we do for a living." It is the work of the Christian. It is the Christian profession. It is the job of the church member; it is what the member does. It is the primary occupation of those who have dedicated their life to the mission of Jesus Christ.

The Christian vocation, then, is the response by the individual member to the gift of God's love. It is faith in the fact that in God's love we are freed and open to the possibility of becoming a proclaimer, healer, and server in the spirit of Jesus' ministry.

We see in the crucifixion and the resurrection of Jesus Christ both God's willingness to seek us out and Jesus' obedience to the will of God. It is in this image that we understand what is meant by the word **incarnation.** The vocation we seek, like the life of Jesus Christ, is a life dedicated to obedience and to being God's presence in the world. It is the incarnation of God's will in our human response.

• ***The Aaronic priesthood as proclaimer:*** The proclamation is of the good news. The good news is that the love of God transforms ordinary life into something extraordinary. Jesus' life—his presence among those who followed him—transformed the nature of their lives and sent them seeking an unimaginable but longed-for future. Jesus preached the message of good news to those who were helpless and broken.

The authors of the New Testament tell us that Jesus came to preach the Word. But we have come to understand that preaching, in this case, does not mean simply that Jesus delivered his message to the masses. The role of proclaimer was more complicated than that. It was a life of presentation that required more than simply speaking. Jesus proclaimed the good news of the gospel through the events of his life. He carried out God's intentions through being available and by being mercifully open to those who lived outside the community of the "righteous": to the poor, the diseased, and the sinner. In his death and resurrection, Jesus Christ proclaimed the vindication of all he had taught and done.

When we say "the...word was made flesh, and dwelt among us" (John 1:14), we are inclined to think of the divine nature of Jesus' creation. But there is more than that involved, for Jesus' life was, and is, an affirmation that God lives with the people of the community. The significance of incarnation is found in the degree that the divine message was proclaimed in the way Jesus lived out his life. It is also true that our strongest proclamation lies in our willingness to live our lives as models of the good news of Jesus Christ.

The proclamation made by and through Jesus Christ is that God is love, that God is involved in the lives of all individuals, and that the promise of the kingdom is for all people. For us then to be proclaimers, we must learn to live the life incarnate: to be a living expression of the fact that God is love, to be involved in the lives of all people, and to be the true manifestation of the Spirit that promises that the kingdom is for everyone. We affirm that we have come to know of Jesus Christ by the fact that this knowledge has changed, illuminated, and motivated our lives.

Maurice A. Fetty writes, "For one thing Jesus' teaching was new because it involved *commitment, not just comment.*" He recalls for us the old joke about a lecture being a process in which the information in the professor's notes passes to the students' notebooks without going through the minds of either. That is not the case when one professes the "Good News," for it is not communicated if the proclamation does not come from the soul of the teacher and does not touch the heart of the learner.[3]

Amid the great information onslaught of today, we discover that something becomes significant to us when the teacher professes what has changed his or her life; the message becomes meaningful in the testimony of the professor. In a very real way "the medium becomes the message."

The affirmation of the proclaimer is seen in what Duane Couey, who served as a member of the First Presidency and as presiding evangelist, used to call "incarnational theology." Our call is not to withdraw into ourselves, to be a special and isolated people. Jesus threw himself into the business of living; he involved himself in every aspect of life. What this says is that the people of God are called not to incorporate the wickedness but to overcome it, sharing ourselves with the people of the world and relating our lives to overcoming the problems we find.

Another way for us to consider the Aaronic priesthood member as proclaimer is to consider the word **messenger.** The Aaronic priesthood has long been associated with what many call the ministry of angels. The Presiding Bishopric addressed the meaning of this relationship at the 1994 World Conference and, in doing so, addressed this concept of messenger. Angelic ministry, as we have come to understand it, is the ministry of "the message" just as it is the ministry of "presence." We can do little better than to quote a brief passage here:

> ...the ministry of angels is associated with the peaceful acceptance of the decisions of God that are reflected in our lives—sometimes joyfully and sometimes with great sadness—but always with the promise of God's care....
>
> The key to such ministry of presence already lies within the purview of the Aaronic priesthood by virtue of their calling to family ministry, conflict resolution, teaching of stewardship principles, and as representatives of the body of Christ to those in need of the assurance of God's love.[4]

Using this term "messenger," it is enlightening to see the Aaronic priesthood function as providers of the gift of message, in the same manner that they are providers of the gift of presence. They are, as we have considered, professors of the Good News which so many have never known or have, unfortunately, forgotten.

• *The Aaronic priesthood as healer:* Perhaps at no time has the role of healing been so significant as it is today. In our ever more complicated life, the isolation of the weary, the maimed, and the brokenhearted is increasingly apparent. Such people, often aware only of their uneasiness, are nevertheless deeply in need of help. Never, it seems, has the fragmentation of human life been so obvious nor have the usual methods of renewal appeared so ineffective. What the world needs is the healing ministry that is found in the affirmation of God's concern for human wholeness.

The life and ministry of Jesus provide us with what it means to be a healer, for it models the healing process—a process that can be envisioned by an attitude of personal commitment. Such a vision includes the ability to recognize the nature of sickness, both in individuals and in the society that surrounds us. On our part it requires a willingness to make the effort to understand the nature of the sickness and its roots. And it assumes our willingness to understand what is required of us if we are to initiate healing. It also assumes our readiness to respond to what is needed in the healing process.[5]

The key to healing as Jesus proclaimed it is in the reordering, that is, restructuring of life. Such a healing begins when one recognizes the faith of the healer. The act of healing begins with the realization of human and divine concern, a concern that is the first balm for isolation. Such healing is the process of allowing people to recapture their essential selves, to be the person they were created to be.

So often the source of the alienation—of the isolation—lies in a lack of faith. Thus the healing art is often no more difficult to define, or no harder to accomplish, than to recognize a lack of faith. It is the task of the healer, as it was Jesus' task, to be the instrument through which such faith is restored. And in the restoration, the act of healing proclaims the person whole.

• *The Aaronic priesthood as server:* This brings us back again to the fact that priesthood is service. But what is the nature of that service? When Jesus responded to the questions of the disciples, he uncovered one of the most difficult of all the instructions we have received from our Lord. "If any[one] desire to be first," he said, "[they] shall be last of all, and servant of all" (Mark 9:32).

It is a call for other-directed love and for unconditional giving.

The nature of this love, and our response to it, is so beautifully expressed in the hymn "Take My Life and Let It Be."

Take my life and let it be Consecrated, Lord, to thee;
Take my moments and my days; Let them flow in ceaseless praise.
Take my hands, my feet, my love; At thine impulse let them move;
Take my voice and let me sing Always, only, for my King.

Take my silver and my gold; Naught of thine would I withhold;
Take my heart, my mind, my will; Let them be thy servants still.
Take my love; my Lord, I pour At thy feet its treasure store;
Take myself, and I will be Ever, only, all for thee. Amen.[6]

We are called to serve the world for, and in response to, God—and to do so as an unconditional expression of the love we received from God.

There is often some confusion about the much quoted scriptural comment, "If any[one] desire to be first...." Some have chosen to interpret it to mean that our service will make us number one. In a larger view of the message of Jesus Christ, this does not seem to be what is suggested. "First" as it is used here means "ahead," or as leader, example, or model to follow. If you would be the one to lead, to direct others to the path of the gospel and into the chambers of the kingdom, then you must first learn to serve. People will not follow, nor will they listen, if the very nature of your life does not affirm what you believe.

Such a role—the concept of personal mission—requires the fundamental qualities of insight, courage, and humility. One source describes this insight:

> Our calling, and therefore our response, becomes specific as we insightfully determine where, with whom, and how we are called to act in partnership with God.... The disciple who embarks on mission with God does so with an openness to ever-expanding insight into God's ways and the lives of those who are touched.[7]

Likewise, it takes courage for the individual to accept, and to act on, God's revelation in their lives. In the beginning there may well be the tendency to feel unworthy, that the calling is beyond us, and that it is an act of courage, as well as of faith, to accept this responsibility and act on it.

Humility helps us reflect on the limited role we play in the larger plan of the Good News. Humility is, paradoxically, the willingness to be open to God's call and response.

Paul M. Edwards

Notes

1. *Guidelines for Priesthood: Ordination, Preparation, Continuing Commitment* (Independence, Missouri: Herald House, 1985), 7.
2. For further comments on the role of discipleship, see Maurice A. Fetty, *Putting Your Life on the Line: Seven Sermons for the Lenten/Easter Season* (Nashville, Tennessee: Abingdon Press, 1979), 23–33.
3. Ibid., 13–14.
4. H–18 "Report on Ministry of Angels," *World Conference Bulletin 1994* (Saturday, April 9, 1994): 281.
5. David P. Premoe and David R. Jewell, *Christian Vocation: The Call to Respond to the Gift of God's Love* (Independence, Missouri: Pastoral Service Commission, 1979), 74.
6. *Hymns of the Saints* (Independence, Missouri: Herald House, 1981), 408.
7. Charles Mader, Peter Judd, and Bruce Jones, *All Are Called* (Independence, Missouri: Herald House, 1984), 71.

CHAPTER 2

A Brief History of Aaronic Quorums

Since the beginnings of the Restoration, the term **priesthood** has been used synonymously with authority. Like so much of what we understand about the religious movement that began in Palmyra, New York, in the 1820s, there has been an evolution: who we are today is considerably different from what we once were. The needs of an emerging faith group, as perceived by the leadership, were prompted by divine inspiration and provided the impetus for this evolution. Within the history of priesthood authority and the Aaronic order can be found the evolution of our church institution.

Few records on priesthood development are extant from the early years for at least two reasons: during those years the church was frequently uprooted and so much of the church's transactions simply were not recorded. Many assumptions will be necessary during this exploration of the Aaronic priesthood's past. Influences prompting the historical development of priesthood can be understood with relative accuracy, because the origins date back to the foundational event of the Book of Mormon translation.

During the arduous process of translating the Book of Mormon, Joseph Smith, Jr., and Oliver Cowdery became very sensitive to the need for baptism. Their concern may have originated from their translated ac-

27

count in III Nephi explaining the origins of the church in ancient America. One issue, among the many that they immediately confronted, was of authority to administer the sacraments. With this concern weighing heavily upon them, they sought divine counsel. In 1834, Cowdery recorded that an angel of God appeared and bestowed on them the priesthood after the order of Aaron. The angel said, "Upon you my fellow servants, in the name of the Messiah I confer this priesthood and this authority, which shall remain upon earth, that the sons of Levi may yet offer an offering unto the Lord in righteousness!"[1]

Joseph Smith, Jr., provided a more detailed account eight years later.[2] He recorded the date of the visitation as May 15, 1829, and identified the angel as John the Baptist. Smith also stated that the messenger acted under the authority of Peter, James, and John. After being set apart to the Aaronic priesthood, Joseph and Oliver were then commissioned to baptize and ordain each other. Neither account mentioned the specific location of the actual baptism, though it is reasonable to think that the baptisms would have taken place in the Susquehanna River near Harmony, Pennsylvania. Also neither account mentioned the specific priesthood office to which they were ordained. This omission is understandable. By this early date, the church institution had not been created, and particular priesthood functions were not clearly understood or defined.

The formulation of a priesthood theology for Joseph Smith, Jr., appeared to evolve during the translation of the Book of Mormon. Completion of the project coincided with the baptism and ordination of the two founders in 1829. Most priesthood offices were inscribed in the ancient writings, including high priest, priest, teacher, and occasionally elder; however, bishop, deacon, seventy, or evangelist-patriarch were not. Priesthood responsibilities were only generally mentioned, with little distinction made between offices.

Indeed, the Book of Mormon makes no distinction between the two orders of priesthood. Reference to an Aaronic priesthood order was not mentioned in the Book of Mormon. In Alma 10, Melchisedec, king of Salem, exercised mighty faith during the difficult times when his people "had waxed strong in iniquity and abominations."[3] He received the office of the high priesthood according to the holy order of God.

It is possible, however, to trace the origins of the Aaronic priesthood in the modern day through the revelations recorded in the Doctrine and Covenants. In April 1829 at Harmony, Pennsylvania, a revelation through Smith identified the gift of Aaron in Oliver Cowdery.[4] Though not specifically mentioned, using Aaron as a model, this could be the beginning of the Restoration process of establishing the Aaronic priesthood. The first recordings of priesthood, in revelation, occurred in June 1829 at Fayette, New York, when Oliver Cowdery and David Whitmer (probably accompanied by Martin Harris, thus bringing together the "three witnesses") were chosen to select the first apostles in the Twelve.[5] The Twelve were challenged to go into all the world to preach the gospel, to walk uprightly and not sin, and to ordain priests and teachers to declare the gospel. Differentiation among the offices and orders of priesthood had not yet developed. Specific priesthood responsibilities for the different offices became a focus in Section 17.

The first reference to the Aaronic priesthood came in the revelation of March 28, 1835, Section 104, through Joseph at Kirtland, Ohio.[6] As the charter members of the

Twelve were preparing for their first mission as a quorum of apostles, they asked for divine counsel concerning their comfort and duty as God's special witnesses. Contained within the comprehensive revelatory response were specific guidelines for organization and tasks of the numerous priesthood offices. Here, the relationship of the priesthood orders was established, with the Melchisedec as the "higher" and the Aaronic as the "lesser" order (Doctrine and Covenants 104:9a, 10). Certainly, church leaders made some distinction between the two orders, because, in 1833, the plans for the Kirtland Temple provided for separate seating of the Aaronic and Melchisedec priesthoods. In the opening statement of the revelation, the Aaronic priesthood was identified as the Levitical priesthood. "Levitical" referred to the tribe of Levi who were designated to perform the "lower services of the tabernacle and temple" and were special servants of the Lord.[7] These responsibilities were conferred on Aaron, the brother of Moses. Levites had numerous important functions. They were to be the "interpreters of the Law when it was read in the public assemblies" for the purpose of teaching the entire community of believers.[8]

Joseph Smith, Jr., interpreted the divine instruction as directing the Aaronic priesthood to hold the keys to the ministering of angels and to administer the outward ordinances. These included the letter of the gospel and baptism of repentance for the remission of sins. The presidency of the Aaronic priesthood resided with the bishopric. Edward Partridge, as the first bishop with presiding responsibilities, also became the first president of the Aaronic priesthood.[9]

When the church reorganized at Amboy, Illinois, and officially located at Plano, Illinois, the church leadership recognized the need to continue priesthood authority. Though Joseph III spoke and wrote very little on Aaronic ministry and priesthood authority, William H. Kelley (1841–1915), for many years one of the leading ministers of the Reorganization, wrote his important book: Presidency and Priesthood: The Apostacy, Reformation and Restoration (1890). Kelley offered a comprehensive Old Testament survey of the origins of both priesthood orders, adding to the Reorganized Church's understanding. Roy A. Cheville continued this tradition by identifying authority as power and competency in a series of six lectures delivered to the priesthood in Independence on January 8–13, 1956.[10] Though specifically presented to the Melchisedec order, his thoughts were appropriate for all priesthood to accept as a challenge the responsibility to speak and act on behalf of God. This understanding, according to Cheville, was not static, but continued to evolve: "The enduring basics of [our] movement need to be reinterpreted expandingly in the thought patterns of our dynamic culture."[11] The dynamic nature of the Aaronic ministry, so evident through the ages, endures.

In common to both orders of priesthood is the historic call to service, as Aaronic priesthood ministry makes its valuable contribution to both members and friends of the church. Ordained of God, Aaronic ministers find a rich heritage guided by the Holy Spirit. The call is to go forth among the people, ministering as did Aaron. What was begun at the time of Aaron and restored in 1829, continues today.

Mark A. Scherer

Notes

1. In a letter to W. W. Phelps written by Oliver Cowdery (with the collaboration of Joseph Smith) in the Kirtland, Ohio, *Latter Day Saints' Messenger and Advocate* 1, no. 1 (October 1834): 16.
2. Joseph Smith, "History of Joseph Smith," *Times and Seasons* 3, no. 19 (August 1, 1842): 865–866.
3. Alma 10: 11.
4. Doctrine and Covenants 8: 3b.
5. Doctrine and Covenants 16: 5, 6.
6. Doctrine and Covenants 104: 1a.
7. F. Henry Edwards, *A New Commentary on the Doctrine and Covenants* (Independence, Missouri: Herald House, 1977), 375.
8. Bernhard W. Anderson, *Understanding the Old Testament*, 3rd ed. (Englewood Cliffs, New Jersey: Prentice-Hall, 1986), 495.
9. Doctrine and Covenants 104:40.
10. Roy A. Cheville, *By What Authority* (Independence, Missouri: Herald House, 1956).
11. Ibid., 9.

CHAPTER 3

Survey of Aaronic Educational Activities

From the early days of the church, the Aaronic priesthood was associated with **competence** and **morale.** Ministers of this focus must know how to reach and help people and should feel capable of doing so. At stake were hard realities about whether the people would be well grounded in the basics of church life. Attention to the maintenance of those basics was the specialized concern of Aaronic ministry.

At its best, of course, the church's understanding of competence and morale always touches on spiritual stamina as well as training and education. As a young church it could not rely on a long-established tradition in theology and ministerial practicum. Ministers were selected from those at hand, singling out under the impress of the Spirit those who seemed capable of grasping the call to ministry and who seemed to know how—or at least were willing to learn how—to do well what must be done in consort with other ministers.

As the church accumulated a more formal structure, special responsibility for the competence and morale of the Aaronic ministry fell on the Bishopric. Many kinds of educational and motivational resources have been available over the years, as can be seen by exploring the history of quorums and similar activities. In the last half century, the Presiding Bishopric has taken very seriously the role of Aaronic competence and morale. Many of us will remember the concerns of G. Leslie DeLapp, Walter N. Johnson, Francis E. Hansen, Gene M. Hummel, and Norman E. Swails. In each case these leaders, along with their associate bishops at headquarters and in the field, worked so that Aaronic ministers could pursue excellence and enjoy self-confidence and respect.

Increasingly, specialized educational programs and resources have come to play a vital part. In our earlier history are such reminders as the functions (even the physical structure) of the Kirtland Temple. In the twentieth century, we remember that the School of the Restoration included a specific focus on Aaronic education, with staff relationship to the Bishopric. When Temple School was organized, its constitution included special staff roles and programs to provide a continuing relationship with the Bishopric in the pursuit of Aaronic education.

During Temple School's earlier years, there was a specific Aaronic Education and Training arm that worked directly under the Presiding Bishopric, even though maintaining close relationship with Temple School. This Bishopric office was directed by Jerry C. Runkle, who soon became known as "Mister Aaronic" for his aggressive development of programs and course materials and his general advocacy of Aaronic excellence. In Temple School, Lyman F. Edwards, who served as director of field schools, became responsible to honor the "dotted line" with the Bishopric and to incorporate the programs and course materials of the Bishopric's Aaronic office within the overall field school structure.

The field school program of Temple School, including the Aaronic aspect, grew beyond expectation. An important factor in this was the interest and hard work of stake and regional bishops, who represented the Aaronic program as bishops, but also related to Temple School in planning and implementing specific field school experiences. Jerry Runkle and Lyman Edwards worked closely to achieve this growth and mutual access while maintaining high standards of both offices, with exceptional support from Francis Hansen, William T. Higdon, and Geoffrey Spencer (which continued unabated from their successors Gene Hummel and Paul M. Edwards).

During budget challenges, some economies were pursued while attempting to preserve the strength of Aaronic education. Lyman Edwards was transferred to work full time with Jerry Runkle in the Aaronic office, enjoying continued cooperation and access at Temple School through Paul Edwards and other staff there. When Jerry Runkle retired, Lyman Edwards returned to Temple School as director of field schools but retained the role of director of Aaronic education. In all of this there were some economy measures, such as curtailment of the *Aaronic Newsletter*; but the Aaronic field work grew and prospered. When Lyman Edwards retired, Paul Edwards and other Temple School staff, with help from the Bishopric arm (such as the continuing Aaronic Education committee of the Order of Bishops) maintained the Aaronic focus within Temple School.

The work of the church in Aaronic educational activities has been an encouraging success story. Grateful recognition should be extended at least at these points:

• *To field bishops,* in stake, regional, and other roles, who worked hard and in good spirit to bring courses and program advantages to their areas. Some bishops made Aaronic concerns a major part of their ministry.

• *To the field administrators and Temple School leaders,* who included Aaronic concerns in planning and implementing field school experiences. Some local leaders went to great lengths to promote Aaronic as well as other educational successes.

• *To Aaronic ministers,* who have supported Temple School/Aaronic Ministry field schools. Time and time again certain key familiar faces showed up in field school classes. Some learners took special pleasure in enrolling for every new course offering or in driving hundreds of miles for a session or otherwise going above and beyond. And many class members (not always Aaronic ministers) brought insight and high expectation, not only by their attendance, but by their helpful critiques.

• *To headquarters' leaders,* whether serving in presiding, educational, Bishopric, or other roles, who willingly cooperated and melded energies in the pursuit of high quality education for Aaronic ministers. Leaders at all levels of church administration have in recent years honored each other across the boundaries of lines and levels.

Genuine education (thorough and thoughtful), as well as training and other resources toward effective ministry, surely will continue to occupy the energies of the church. And certainly education for Aaronic ministers remains a high priority. Absolutely nothing can replace the competence and confidence that comes from good education. As a fully in-touch religious entity, the church will continue to provide resources to equip Aaronic ministers for the openings that abound for extending servant ministry in our contemporary world.

Lyman F. Edwards

CHAPTER 4

Aaronic Ministry and the Temple

*I was hungry and you formed a humanities club
to discuss my hunger.*
Thank you.

*I was imprisoned and you crept off quietly
to your chapel to pray for my release.*
Nice.

*I was naked and in your mind you debated the
morality of my appearance.*
What good did that do?

*I was sick and you knelt and thanked God
for your health.*
But I needed you.

*I was homeless and you preached to me of the
shelter of the love of God.*
I wish you'd taken me home.

I was lonely and you left me alone to pray for me.
Why didn't you stay?

*You seem so holy, so close to God;
But I'm still very hungry, lonely, cold,
and still in pain.*
Does it matter?[1]

Yes, it matters. It matters to Christians generally and, more specifically, it matters to members of the Aaronic quorums. For it falls to the Aaronic ministers to make the primary response to such human questions and needs. One place where these needs are so clearly found is among those who come to the Temple to visit and to worship.

There are many visitors to the Temple on any given day. Some are on business to service the building and its people's needs. Some people come consumed with their own deep, personal needs. Some come simply as tourists to view the awesome architecture of the building. Some are employees of the World Church who pass in and about the Temple area as a part of their daily tasks. Others we could simply classify as fellow Christians here to seek and offer affirmation and unity.

For each of these individuals there is a need; for each, an opportunity for service.

The Purpose of Temple Ministries

Instructions recorded in Doctrine and Covenants 156:5a identify the Temple as being dedicated to the pursuit of peace, and for reconciliation and healing of the spirit. The Temple was built in response to the need to care. As Christians we are called to listen, to love, and to care for others as Jesus did. Unlike Moses who had a list of many commandments to consider, Jesus gave us but one primary law: to love one another. The Temple, if it is to fulfill its mission as recorded in the Doctrine and Covenants, must be a place of extraordinary love and care.

God has loved me, so have I loved you; continue you in my love.

If you keep my commandments, you shall live in my love; even as I have kept God commandments, and abide in the love of God.

These things have I spoken unto you, that my joy might remain in you, and that your joy might be full.

This is my commandment, That you love one another, as I have loved you.

Greater love hath no one than this, that a person lay down their life for their friends.

—adapted from John 15:9–13

We can safely assume that people coming into the Temple, regardless if they are members of the Restoration or not, reflect the cross-section of society. Thus we must assume they are in need of the Good News of God: the news of hope and renewal. People throughout the world are in need of such help. Their souls and bodies are broken with the heaviness of living.

Christians have been given the gift of responsibility—to provide others with the healing balm of affirmation, to bear their burdens, and to heal with love. This is not to be done on a part-time basis if and when convenient; this is a call to continuous service.

The story is told of a shopper who paid for a purchase. The clerk immediately turned to help someone else but had failed to provide a bag for the items. Another clerk, standing nearby, was asked by the shopper for a sack. The second clerk, with a look of utter disbelief, shook her head saying cryptically, "But it's not my shift yet." For Aaronic ministries, there are no shifts, no time-outs, no breaks; only human beings in need of love.

Caring

To care is to help provide growth and actualize the worth of self and others. Caring gives a comprehensive meaning and order to life. The major ingredients of actualizing and caring are to understand needs and properly respond with real intent, not phoniness.

Let love be without dissimulation. Abhor that which is evil and cleave to that which is good. Be kindly affectioned one to another with...love; in honor preferring one another.—Romans 12:9,10

Our world has lost the capacity for reverence, loneliness drains joy from our lives, and we lose touch with ourselves and others. People have basic needs such as food, clothing, and shelter. But people have other needs, too: to be loved, cared about, and feel worthy of self-esteem.

Theology is talking about God. Religion is experiencing God. Many people will view the Temple as a sight-seeing tour, but the building alone will not bring these people closer to Christ. Only another human being will bring them to Christlike ways. Aaronic ministers should first be involved in educating themselves in preparation for their service in Temple ministries. Just as each person cares for his or her body, home, and belongings, they should also care for their mind, spirit, and outreach.

There are many opportunities for learning available through the Temple. The services available to prepare an individual are numerous. Some of these include teaching, guiding, research, ushering, chaplaincy, museum attendant, receptionist, guide, visit consultant, and others. An Aaronic minister identifies his or her special gift and calling. This is a personal search to discover a ministry that is unique and special.

If that calling is financial watchcare, then preparation through coursework, experience, and community education is of primary importance. If the ministry to be offered is one of welcoming, then attention to personal habits such as grooming, contact with others, and interactive qualities will be upheld. If leadership is an asset, then continual updating of information, practice in speaking, and presence ministry will be fostered. Once identified as a possibility to be explored, a minister may move forth in their ministry to others. These gifts often change and interact as we are associated with others in ministry. Even Jesus' ministry was varied and was concentrated in different areas at various times of his life.

Balcony People

The ministry of the Aaronic priesthood should always be united in inspiring others. This is what Joyce Landorf Heatherley identifies in the term **balcony people.** In our minds, there are also **basement people** who damage personhood with comments of inferiority and abuse. Aaronic priesthood especially should be identified as balcony people who give strength, courage, and confidence. They offer nurture, service, and caring to those in need, whatever the need may be. In fact, the specific need often may not be known—only that there is a need.

Some people come to the Temple to seek healing. They are missing vital elements of a fulfilling life. They need affiliation, safety, acceptance, spirituality, prayer, and meditation. They need the caring of another human. They do not come for the corporate ritual of worship, but to be touched, to share, and to explore the depths of their lives.

The top of the spiral cannot be seen from the inside of the sanctuary. This is fitting symbolism as we also cannot see the inside depths of another's soul. We cannot tell them who to be. We are called to affirm them in their own experience on the journey. They ask us to hear what they are not saying and to see what they cannot express.

In ministry we can attempt to see the real person, to look behind the glazed eyes, to see behind the masks of politeness and protocol. Our world is so afraid to touch others physically and spiritually. What is *proper* contact? A firm handshake, a hug, a pat on the back or shoulder, and, most importantly, eye contact. We have become so afraid of touching others that we do not even attempt to touch for fear that we might be rejected. Aaronic ministers should risk making contact with those afraid to ask and yet seeking. Christianity is a personal conviction in a communal faith.

Temple Worship Opportunities

A variety of worship settings are available in the Temple for individuals and groups. Aaronic ministry is provided on a personal level with others through consultation, guidance, meditation, prayer, study, and the sacraments.

There are also opportunities to provide ministry with more than one person. This may be in the form of corporate worship, prayer, music, or other service. All worship in the Temple should reflect the collective "we" of our Christianity. We pray for all humanity in the Daily Prayer for Peace.

The diversity of other religious organizations prompts a cooperation of community as others share in the expressions of Temple ministries. The use of the facilities for many functions fosters a special relationship to share the unique ministry of Aaronic priesthood members.

Caring Enough to Act

In the story of the Good Samaritan, all those who passed by the injured man did not care enough to stop and help. They probably cared, but not enough to act. However, the Samaritan saw the need of another person and cared, and actively set out to help in a verbal, nonverbal, financial, and physical way. Jesus gave the formula for Aaronic ministry: to care for others is the measure of greatness. When we as ministers care enough to minister to ourselves, others, and the community, we are truly providing the full meaning of Temple ministry.

The following expresses the heart of Aaronic ministry.

In Other People's Shoes
(Romans 12:15)

Lord, your love increases my sensitivity
to needy people in today's world.

I bring my prayers to you:
for those who suffer pain;
for those whose minds are disturbed;
for brilliant people who waste their abilities;
for those with great potential
   but who lack the opportunity to realize it;
for those whose dreams have shattered;
for those who live behind bars;
for those who have been maimed by violence;
for those who have been disgraced and wounded
   by other people's wrongdoing;
for those who have lost a loved one;
for those who are suffering from
   incurable diseases;
for those who face death,
especially those who face it without you.
Help me, Lord, to make myself available
to those who need help,
that in practical and in spiritual ways
I may convey your love to them.[2]

Joni Wilson

Notes

1. Anonymous poem
2. Bryan Jeffery Leech, *Lift My Spirits, Lord* © 1977. All rights reserved. Used by permission of the author.

SECTION II

The Aaronic Offices

CHAPTER 5

Being a Deacon in Today's Church

All Christians are called to live lives of service and commitment. Aaronic priesthood ministry is responsible for the "outward ordinances," that is, the application of the gospel to everyday life. The office of deacon is an expression of this ministry. A deacon is one who leads and teaches a life of service and commitment.

The word **deacon** comes from a Greek word, *diakonos*, meaning "servant." As such, deacons provide servant and stewardship ministry in caring for congregational and member needs. While we are all called to serve each other, the specific role of the deacon is to call the church to this task and to teach the church how this responsibility can be carried out. This is done by leadership and by example.

In *Guidelines for Priesthood*[1] a description is given that cites ways the deacon can demonstrate the gospel in our day-to-day living. Here are those statements:

Qualifications

Deacons are committed to Jesus Christ and the cause of God's kingdom. Priesthood members are to lead clean lives, free from all chemical dependence; they are to be honest, humble, clean, and neat in appearance and walk uprightly before the Lord. They avoid all immoral activ-

47

ity and appearance of evil. Deacons respond affirmatively in their temporal stewardships. They are faithful in church attendance and in their priesthood duties; they should continually seek to magnify their calling.

Supervision

The deacon is a congregational minister and serves under the general guidance of the pastor of the congregation or anyone the pastor may delegate for a specific purpose. The deacon may assist teachers, priests, and elders in their duties as requested.

Specific Duties of Office

1. The deacon is concerned with the physical welfare of church members and their families.

1.1 The deacon identifies closely with the poor, the sick, the helpless and needy, and assists them in every way possible to meet their needs. The deacon is their advocate and presents their needs to financial officers if financial assistance is required, the pastor and elders for spiritual ministries, the priests and teachers and others for home ministry and friendly visits.

1.2 The deacon identifies community and governmental assistance programs relevant to the physical needs of the poor among the Saints and assists in assuring that their needs are met by the proper agencies.

2. The deacon is concerned with the care, maintenance, and appearance of the properties of the church.

2.1 The deacon is the advocate for the physical properties of the church. The deacon identifies and works to develop adequate programs of cleanliness and maintenance of church property.

2.2 The deacon is concerned with the appearance and contribution of the church property to the neighborhood of which it is a part. Physical appearance, order, and neatness of lawn, signs, and building are of special importance to the deacon.

3. *The deacon is concerned with the physical comfort of the Saints whenever the congregation assembles.*

3.1 The deacon assures cleanliness, order, and proper temperature in the building.

3.2 The deacon assures friendly and orderly ushering and decorum in congregational meetings.

3.3 The deacon receives the offerings in public worship and assures their transmittal to the congregation's financial officers.

3.4 The deacon opens the church for congregational meetings and assures the building's security at the close of meetings.

Ministries the Deacon May Be Requested or Elected to Perform

1. Serve as congregational stewardship commissioner.

2. Serve as member or chair of the church building committee.

3. Serve as member or chair the stewardship commission.

4. Serve as head deacon or usher.

5. Serve as member or president of a deacon's quorum.

6. Assist priests and teachers in home ministry.

7. Teach classes as requested in church school, or other settings.

8. Provide financial management teaching to families and congregation.

9. Visit the homes of Saints with special concern for those in physical need.

General Duties

As a member of the Aaronic priesthood, the deacon is to minister primarily in the congregation, teaching the value of temporalities in personal spiritual development, and serving the temporal needs of the Saints. The deacon and all priesthood are to invite people to come to Christ. They are to teach and encourage people to respond to the gospel of Jesus Christ, and be reconciled to Christ through faith, repentance, baptism, and other gospel principles.[2]

The ministry of the deacon is an essential ingredient in the life and ministry of the church because the deacon provides practical help to members in living their lives "in the light of the gospel" through service and through stewardship commitment.

A deacon is a minister of service and of stewardship. Just as the responsibilities to the church facility (care of the building) is one expression of that ministry, so also is an understanding of stewardship and its practical applications. Stewardship is the responsible use of resources. Tangible resources, such as money, are important in this regard, but the responsible use of one's time, talents, and relationships are also important. Ministry in these areas may involve answering specific questions, sharing ideas, or acting as an advocate in providing information or referrals in order to provide the help that is needed.

In light of this calling, deacons are concerned about providing for the physical care and comfort of the members, both personally and corporately, that is, the church as a whole. This concern may focus on differing needs, including personal, physical, and financial. The deacon may assist in various ways to ensure that such needs are being met.

Congregational and Public Ministries

Whenever the congregation meets together, the deacon is responsible for addressing a variety of needs. Seemingly simple tasks of service symbolize the commitment of the church to care for its members and friends. These tasks include such things as "ushering ministries" (for example, greeting the worshipers, handing out printed orders of service, and maintaining a comfortable environment), as well as assisting during the service and providing effective ministry from the rostrum.

Deacons provide these types of ministry in two ways: taking the initiative in performing tasks themselves and responsibly leading others. Thus by example and by leadership are the needs of the church met.

A deacon may be responsible for a specific worship service as "head deacon" or "head usher." Such responsibility includes greeting the people as they arrive. The deacon may do this or arrange to have "hosts" do the welcoming. Deacons may pass out bulletins themselves or enlist others, such as the youth, to help in this task. Seating of worshipers varies by congregations. Whether people are shown to a seat or invited to seat themselves, there remains an awareness of individual needs as they arise, such as a parent struggling to find a seat while carrying an infant, blanket, and diaper bag, or an elderly person who may have trouble with mobility, seeing, or hearing. Also, there is a tendency for people to sit in the back of the sanctuary. When the congregation is seated toward the front, closer to the rostrum, the quality of the service is enhanced. Deacons may be aware of this natural human tendency and help arrange the seating with the worship planners or "reserve" the back rows for special seating for latecomers.

Ushering also involves responsibility in assisting with the receiving of offerings. This is often incorporated by various methods, depending on traditions and/or the specific worship service. Whatever the case, the offering procedure should be well-planned and thoughtfully executed. The offering is an act of worship and response. Those involved in helping should carry out the receiving of offerings with precision and quiet dignity.

Providing assistance to the smooth functioning of the worship service and its ordinances and sacraments is a vital function of the deacon's ministry. There are many ways the deacon's assistance is necessary, and deacons should be in close communication with the planners and those participating in the services. Activities such as filling the baptismal font and regulating the water temperature, as well as providing for dressing areas, serves those being baptized. For confirmations, ordinations, administrations to the sick, and the blessing of children, seating and microphones should be arranged as needed.

The sacrament of the Lord's Supper also requires a systematic, well-planned approach. Again, the deacon may do some of these tasks or provide for others to assist. The Communion ware and the linens for the Communion table should be clean, and the linens should be pressed. The bread and wine should be prepared in accordance with local custom and placed on the table in a way that will help the blessing and serving to go smoothly. If there are metal covers for the plates and trays, there should be a place to put them when the emblems are uncovered. Have extra bread and wine available, usually at the back of the sanctuary, if needed, and someone able to assist if anything is spilled. When the serving is completed, the plates and trays should be collected quietly and everything cleaned and put away immediately following the service.

Dismissal of the congregation is another part of the service the deacon should be actively aware of. It, too, may vary widely according to need and traditions. Deacons will play an active part in implementation and in evaluating the many needs of the service.

Responsibility and care of the facility is a part of the ministry the deacon exercises. This includes the physical comfort of properly heating and cooling the building during classes and services, as well as lighting needs. Building maintenance, cleaning, and care of the outside area are also important concerns. Again, deacons may be involved in doing some of these tasks themselves, or they may be part of a congregational team, such as the church building commission, which provides leadership and support for such necessary activities.

Stewardship Ministries

Stewardship has its beginnings with the insight that "all things unto me are spiritual" (Doctrine and Covenants 28:9a). For some reason, human beings seem to have the idea that religion is "spiritual" and that the rest of our experience is "temporal." Stewardship is the understanding that all areas of one's life should be managed with a spirit of thanksgiving, reverence, and worship.

The deacon is called to provide ministry as a leader and as an exemplary steward. Deacons can teach others that they see the world in spiritual terms by managing the things that are under their control.

The nature of stewardship is such that it refers to more than the personal management of the resources of an individual or family. Individuals and families live in the context of community, and God's purposes for people living in community is reflected in the concept of Zion. Personal and family stewardship, then, is related to a larger concept of stewardship in which the gifts of God are managed for the benefit of all. The stewardship expressed by individuals and families is a part of the stewardship that all people have over the world in which they live.

Deacons are ministers of stewardship. This incorporates an understanding of the wise use of agency and accountability. To say that agency is an expression of a person's stewardship is to say that important parts of our lives and the lives of others are shaped by the decisions we make.

Because choices make such an important difference in people's lives, people are accountable for their actions and the use of their time, talents, and material resources. Accountability serves two purposes. First, it allows awareness and evaluation of the consequences of decisions. Second, accountability sets the stage for redemption. Not all consequences of decisions are good. The promise of the gospel is that relationships that have been torn by poor stewardship can be mended by the grace of God.

Good stewardship tends to increase the resources that are available to accomplish God's purposes. Good stewardship of financial resources, for example, increases the amount of those resources that can be directed into meaningful endeavors. Good stewardship of time and talents can increase their good use. It is this increase of resources that makes growth possible.

A deacon may have the opportunity to minister to families or individuals experiencing financial difficulties. Financial difficulties can have many causes, and several different kinds of ministry may be appropriate. One common factor is that family financial matters are a sensitive and confidential area and must be handled with tact and confidentiality.

There are three primary causes of financial difficulties in families and individuals. The first is **poor management.** There is a saying that goes, "People do not plan to fail; they fail to plan." People who manage their money poorly often make the mistake of assuming that their problem is inadequate income. The abundance of credit cards in Western society today means that poor managers usually acquire a large indebtedness rather than go without the things they want. Eventually, the burden of the debt is overwhelming, and they are in financial crisis. Consumer credit counseling agencies are available in many communities to help people make arrangements with creditors and salvage their credit.

A second cause of financial difficulty is a temporary **setback.** This occurs when an unusual strain is placed on someone's resources. It may result from loss of a job, prolonged and serious illness or injury, or another major, unexpected factor. Usually we have little control over such events, although careful management in previous years may prepare us better for such crises.

The third cause of financial difficulty is **fixed income** that is too small. This is a special problem for retired people or others who are living on Social Security or some other form of fixed income. It is a long-term problem, and one that is not solved easily. It can also be prevented somewhat by good planning, but the solution to a fixed-income problem after it has occurred may be complicated.

From time to time, a deacon may encounter situations where people need direct financial assistance in the form of gifts or loans. Such assistance is available through the church's Oblation Fund. In local areas, the Oblation Fund is administered by the bishop or stewardship commissioner, who should be contacted before promises of aid are made.

Family Financial Planning

If the deacon is able to educate the congregation on an ongoing basis, fewer crises may arise. There are three major tools of family financial management. First, people with financial problems often do not know how their money is spent. They might be inclined to say, "It just goes." It is not possible to change the way money is spent unless there is some **record of where the money is currently going.** Records do not need to be accurate to the penny, but they should give an accurate picture of the person's spending habits. These records can then be analyzed to discover where changes can be made.

The second major tool is **budgeting.** Budgeting is simply a process of planning how money will be used. It includes planning for savings and retirement as well as for current needs such as food and housing. If people know how their money is spent, they can also plan to change spending habits in constructive ways.

The third tool is **control of expenses.** Once a budget is developed, spending should be controlled to keep within the plan. Good shopping skills, or the ability to get the most value out of a dollar, are essential. A budget and good record-keeping help to keep expenses under control by helping a person know how much money is available for various purposes. People will not feel deprived when they have a sense of commitment and control over their resources. True deprivation comes from the empty feeling people have if they are not in control and lack the spiritual peace that is available to them.

These tools are developed more fully in *Family Financial Planning* by Orval G. Fisher (Herald House, 1992). The church's Financial Development Office and the Stewardship 2000 program information will be of help to the deacon and others in providing effective financial ministry.

Extending the Ministry of the Deacon

The Doctrine and Covenants states that all members of the Aaronic priesthood are to "expound, exhort, and teach" (Doctrine and Covenants, 17:10a, and 11f). These are the primary methods by which priesthood members convey their ministry.

To **expound** is to explain or make plain. For these purposes, it involves the explanation of how the *godspel* (god, good + spel, tale; in other words, the good news of Jesus) is relevant to the Saints' daily lives. It involves the attempt to show how the gospel has meaning and how it transforms every aspect of life. Explaining basic principles of the gospel from the pulpit and answering questions in homes are examples of expounding.

To **exhort** has a similar meaning as "to warn," and they both are subject to dangers of distortion. In their best sense, these concepts mean that the Aaronic priesthood member helps people understand the consequences of their actions. This ministry should help others become aware when their actions and attitudes may have unpleasant or dangerous consequences. People who engage in open criticisms of others, for example, may be creating unnecessary disunity in the congregation. There is always the danger, however, that this task can degenerate into simple finger-pointing. Recognizing the faults of another person is not difficult, and simply pointing them out is not necessarily an act of ministry. Rather, it can be an act of offense that accomplishes nothing other than making someone angry. Exhortation and warning become acts of ministry when they are done by one who is respected and when it is clearly understood to be an act of love. This not only requires careful discernment of faults, but it also requires clear insight into what makes a particular person "tick."

To **teach** is an extension of expounding, exhorting, and warning. It is the ministry of assisting individuals and families to see the true nature of the gospel and to apply it in their lives. It is much more than telling someone what to do. In the ministry of teaching, the deacon takes responsibility not only for presenting information correctly, but also for presenting it in a way that it can be understood and applied by others. It is usually best taught by example. Simply telling people that they should love each other is not teaching unless they are shown what it means.

The deacon's work is ministry in action. Their call is to help put the gospel into action by managing the care of the church facility, by teaching the church about the nature of loving service, and by helping people understand the principles of sound financial management both in their homes and in the church. A deacon's life of service and commitment is part of the call to "invite all to come unto Christ" (Doctrine and Covenants 17:11f). The gospel gives all that the church does its meaning and significance, and the spirit in which deacons carry out their duties gives their proclamation of the gospel a special kind of integrity.[3]

Isleta L. Pement

A. Bruce Lindgren

Notes

1. *Guidelines for Priesthood: Ordination, Preparation, Continuing Commitment* (Independence, Missouri: Herald House, 1985), 80–82; "Plan for Service" (available separately from Membership Records Office, The Auditorium, P.O. Box 1059, Independence, MO 64051).
2. A. Bruce Lindgren, PA101 The Deacon (Independence, Missouri: Temple School Center, 1989), 12–13.
3. For selected resources for ministry of the deacon, please turn to the Bibliography.

CHAPTER 6

Teachers for the Twenty-first Century

Every elder, priest, teacher, or deacon, is to be ordained according to the gifts and callings of God...and is to be ordained by the power of the Holy Ghost.—Doctrine and Covenants 17:12

Introduction

The responsibilities of the teacher are great. This office calls for one with wisdom and genuine love for people. A teacher is a friend, counselor, minister of the Word, and one whose empathy lends strength through understanding and service to others.

Because of the importance of this office and the development of specialized gifts, it is possible that one will spend the balance of their life working in this office. If so, there is no greater calling.

> You who are my disciples must be found continuing in the forefront of those organizations and movements which are recognizing the worth of persons and are committed to bringing the ministry of my Son to bear on their lives.
>
> Working together to this end will promote unity, resolve conflicts, relieve tensions between individuals, and heal the wounds which have been sapping the strength of the church, spiritually and materially. This you must do in the spirit of love and compassion as revealed in my Son during his journey in your midst.—Doctrine and Covenants 151:9–10.

The office of teacher is more an attitude of heart rather than a list of jobs to be performed. Teachers are called to proffer a healing balm on the brokenness within an individual, family, congregation, or community. Teachers are called to model an attitude of love and acceptance. These attitudes are "caught" not "taught." Teachers are not judges keeping track of human failings. Rather, teachers are emissaries of love.

The Teacher Works with Others

The establishment of priesthood with multiple offices is an indication of God's desire that various skills be used in ministry; yet, the development of the total person requires the blending of priesthood talents in a unified effort to minister to an individual's total needs.

It is important that each priesthood office be equipped for its peculiar and unique work. It is equally important that each office recognize the worth of other skilled people who can offer ministry. This may mean referral to professional people, other than those who hold priesthood, who have prepared through academic training to give the assistance required.

The office of teacher is one of the priesthood offices charged with helping people adjust to their social environment and finding the source of spiritual enlightenment and strength through their association with others and in acts of worship. Doctrine and Covenants 17 provides the basic scriptural direction concerning the functions of the Aaronic priesthood offices. It is incumbent on all ordained ministers to supplement their personal skills with training and spiritual growth to face the challenges attendant with their office.

The teacher is the advocate of full participation, healthy relationships, and development of a healing, redeeming attitude among the Saints. If relationships are broken between families or members, the teacher may offer reconciling ministry. This is what "watchcare of the church" means.

The teacher is to promote unity and harmony among the Saints. As a member of the Aaronic priesthood, the teacher is to minister primarily in the congregation, teaching and promoting the benefits of acceptance, understanding, and unity. The teacher, as are all disciples, is to invite people to come to Christ. They are to teach and encourage others to respond to the gospel of Jesus Christ and be reconciled to Christ through faith, repentance, baptism, and other gospel principles.

Teacher: Yesterday, Today, and Tomorrow[1]

What is now Section 17 of the Doctrine and Covenants was called the "Articles and Covenants of the Church of Christ" in the early *Book of Commandments*. This passage was developed by Joseph Smith and Oliver Cowdery to bring together instructions that had been received by the prophet. It was adopted on June 1, 1830, at the first conference of the church. It contains a series of testimonies regarding the establishment of the church, three paragraphs of historical information about the founding of the movement, a statement of basic beliefs, identification of the name of the church, and an outline of the duties of many offices of the priesthood.

This section spells out the role of the Aaronic priesthood in some detail. While there had been a lot of discussion about priesthood roles—even some confusion—it is clearly spelled out here that the role of the Aaronic priesthood is supportive and pastoral. This is not an administrative role. This section affirms that whenever possible priesthood should respond to those functions for which they are primarily responsible. The special role of the teacher is identified as one that should not be interfered with by administrative responsibilities.

During the Reorganization, there is one thread that weaves itself into the tapestry of Aaronic teacher history: the office has always been regarded as important; yet it has been described as being underdeveloped or under-utilized. Joseph Smith III wrote in the *True Latter Day Saints' Herald* in the July 1, 1871, issue a detailed description of his understanding of the Aaronic teacher office, providing the foundation for teacher ministries for the rest of the nineteenth century and into the twentieth century. He wrote:

> It is not difficult to draw a conclusion as to what the general duty of a teacher is; but so much is left unwritten that there are not many who feel themselves fully or even fairly competent to define what are the duties....[2]

The need for an office with the described duties of the Aaronic teacher has always been regarded as important in the life of the church; yet the actual work in the office has often been regarded as falling short of its potential. Most of the *Herald* articles regarding teacher ministry for the next fifty years would be reprints of this article. Joseph Smith III used several images to describe the office: "the constable of the church, the arm of public service, to secure by personal supervision of the saints the performance of their public duties."[3] Joseph went on to give some twenty major facets of teacher ministry, including:

- to know personally every member of the church unto which he is made a standing minister.
- to know whether they are careless...in not attending the meetings of the church...

- to be a pacificator between brethren and sisters who have become estranged by offences...[sic]
- to be the medium through whom wise counsels may prevail...
- to allay fears, dispel doubts, encourage, cheer and comfort any whom he finds drooping and doubtful...
- to arrest the course of the liar by careful reproof...
- to stop by instant rebuke the tongue of the backbiter and the slanderer...
- to refuse to listen, except as a mediator, to any scandalous charge against any one...
- to protect and defend the character of all who are absent when they are assailed...
- the officer to serve "citations to trial" and "summons to attend as witnesses."
- attend the sittings of the councils to serve as a messenger to execute the will of the council.[4]

Joseph's closing statements reflect the ongoing problem the church faced in getting the office of teacher to function effectively within the framework of the other priesthood offices, particularly among elders.

...we think the duties of the office of teacher have been much neglected; and that men have been ordained elders who had more capacity for, and would have made able and wise teachers....

We are still further of the opinion that there are good men who hold the office of teacher, who have been hindered from performing the duties of their office, because of the unwise and uncalled for opposition of elders, who...have unduly repulsed them as teachers, and denied them the privilege of magnifying their calling.[5]

In an 1872 article, Elder Josiah Ells responded to the inquiry of an elder who apparently had the opinion that teachers should not be involved in visiting church members in their homes. Ells attempts to lay out his view that there is nothing in the scriptures or law of the church that would restrict the teacher from visiting "If the priest's duty requires...he shall visit the houses of the saints to enable him to exhort and teach the duties pertaining to the kingdom more perfectly, the teacher's duty may necessitate the same activity."[6] Ells went on to say:

> We regard the teacher then, in the internal economy of the branch, as its chief officer; he it is that is the pacificator; the rebuker of the slanderer, the liar, and the backbiter; bringing the evil doer before the judge; strengthening the hands of them that hang down; confirming the hope of the faint; strengthening the saints in all their trials of sorrow and of faith.[7]

Early Twentieth Century to Modern Times

A preliminary examination of articles published in priesthood journals before World War II does not reveal any major shift in thinking or practice in teacher ministry as outlined by Joseph Smith III, except perhaps a greater emphasis on being a minister of reconciliation and less on being a "police officer."

In the August 24, 1910, *Saints' Herald*, Joseph Smith III responded to a letter from an Aaronic teacher asking for "an outline of a teacher's duty, as you see it."[8] Joseph Smith III listed duties of the office very similar to his 1871 article, except that more care was taken to warn the Aaronic teacher: "He should do this without becoming a busybody, a Paul Pry or impertinent meddler in the affairs of the brethren."

In "Suggestions to Teachers" Charles Fry declared:

> ...the teachers as a class have not met the demands of the work to the extent that they might have been met and should have been met. Nor are the teachers alone responsible for this condition, but the body as a whole. The underestimation is common to the whole membership, and until the place of the teacher, and the comparative importance of his duties, are properly recog-

nized by the membership, his work will be beneath the standard set forth in the law.[9]

Roles and Responsibilities[10]

There is no question that the members of the Aaronic priesthood, like those of the Melchisedec, share many common responsibilities. To some degree their work is interchangeable. But there are also peculiar roles—roles unique to their calling. Teacher responsibilities seem to be of particular importance as the church focuses its attention on the Temple and its role in reconciliation and peacemaking.

Watchcare

Teachers are responsible for the participation, health, and meaningful relationships of the members of the church—all members certainly, but most particularly members of their own congregations. They are called on to promote and produce a healing, redeeming attitude among the membership.

The teacher is often the attendance officer of the congregation, but not like we might think of at school, to force attendance or to punish those who fail to attend regularly. Rather it is the teacher who keeps track of members of the congregation in order to be of assistance to them, to call, visit, or send them a note to be sure they are all right and that they know what is happening in the congregation and to be sure they know they are loved and missed.

Reconciliation

It is also the responsibility of the teacher to act when members of the congregation have conflicts. The teacher does not need to feel constrained to supply all the ministry needed but rather to be alert to the need itself and to help others in the healing process. Often the presence of someone who cares is what is most needed.

Association

It has been suggested that the most distinctive feature of the assignment of the teacher is to "see that the church meet together often" (Doctrine and Covenants 17:11b). This means that the teacher is to see that the members of a given congregation come together often, that they do so in the Spirit of the Master who calls them to service, and that they manage to do so free of conflicts and confrontations. The teacher's role is to minimize the gossiping, the hard feelings, and the negative attitudes of the community so that the members can come together in supportive and constructive tasks. The responsibility for preparing those members, in heart and in mind, may well be the partial task of elders and priests, but the teacher is called on to see to it that the positive community meets and becomes a source of power for itself.

Safety Net

Teachers are called to encourage members to participate in the life of the congregation and to be a motivating factor in providing home ministry to the lonely, help to the shut-in, and support to the single person. To put it briefly, the teacher is to be sure that in the complexities of congregational life, no one is overlooked. In this service, it is the responsibility of the teacher to be aware of what the church offers, what community services are available, and to help members of the congregation find help when they need it.

While the general message to the teacher is to watch over the church and to promote unity and harmony among the Saints, it reflects an ever-broader attitude of help and presence. The role of the teacher is to be there when someone is needed. Others, certainly, should be aware of this as well. But in our busy world even care and kindness sometimes fall between the cracks. At times when everyone intends to help, no one does. It is the calling of the teacher to ensure that this never happens. And as such it is a wonderful and highly significant calling.

Shepherds of God's Flock

Aaronic priesthood responsibilities are identified as local ones—local in the sense they are temporal and are directly related to the immediate needs of the Saints as they assemble. This means that members of the Aaronic priesthood are concerned about the people in ways that are concrete and visible. In effect the Aaronic priesthood serves as sort of a "shepherding ministry." In the Gospel of John (10:12–14) Jesus uses a parable in which he affirms that the shepherd is

> not as a hireling, whose own the sheep are not, who seeth the wolf coming, and leaveth the sheep, and fleeth; and the wolf catcheth the sheep and scattereth them. For I am the good shepherd, and know my sheep, and am known of mine. But he who is a hireling fleeth, because he is a hireling, and careth not for the sheep.

The shepherd is not working for pay. This person is not someone whose rewards are different than those of the sheep, or someone who is acting only for his or her own sake. Rather, a shepherd, as Jesus saw the role, finds that his or her life is tied with that of the flock. Whatever the rewards, they are related to the well-being of those for whom the shepherd is responsible. At the bottom line, the shepherd exists for the flock.

Expound, Warn, Exhort, and Teach

Addressing teacher ministry, the Doctrine and Covenants (17:11f) instructs members of the Aaronic priesthood to expound, warn, exhort, and teach. These are the means by which the priesthood functions. To look a little more closely at these:

- "To expound" is to make clear or clarify, to state or interpret, and thus the members are called on to help in the clarification not only of the gospel but of the local statements of it.
- "To warn" in this sense means to help people understand the consequences of their actions. It is not a threat being made but rather a reading of the situation and presentation of the outcome if things are not changed.
- "To exhort" is a kind of warning but means more than that; it also means to appeal in such a manner that the thing you are afraid will happen does not come about. It carries the sense of preventing disaster by the strong appeal and argument against that which might cause harm.
- "To teach" means to convey information, to show or instruct in such a way that it is possible for people to see the outcome of lives lived under the influence, and in the presence, of Jesus Christ.

While all Aaronic priesthood share these responsibilities, the role of the teacher is specialized. The genius of this division of labor encourages different offices and different responsibilities within the church to focus on the various needs brought to the church by its people.

Peacemaker in Residence

When the office of teacher is considered, the word **peacemaker** quickly comes to mind. The teacher is involved in a variety of ministerial functions but the most difficult revolves around the ministry of reconciliation. As much as the Saints try to be peaceful and loving people, it is the nature of groups to have conflict and even dissension. When people feel strongly about something, as most do about religion, they tend to have their feelings easily hurt. They can be upset by even the best intentions of others. It is human nature to have our own self-interests in mind and to worry more than is necessary about our "rights." It is the particular responsibility of the teacher to address these questions in such a way as to keep human differences from getting in the way of the mission of the church.

The Role of the Aaronic Teacher[11]

It is suggested that there are at least four areas of specialized ministries in the role of teacher. A person may be involved more in one area than another because of his or her gifts and interests. However, no one person can be expected to meet all of these needs. These areas are based on scripture (Doctrine and Covenants 17:11), tradition, and anticipated needs within the RLDS Church.

• *Presence Ministry.* Involves watching attendance patterns, greeting members and visitors, enfolding people into the care of the church, encouraging participation; keeping in touch with inactive or semiactive members; knowing what is happening in a person's life, their character and personal needs; visiting the sick, the homebound, and those in prison.

• *Human Development Ministry.* Assists members and friends to explore their own feelings about themselves, their families, their church, and their life goals. Helps to build positive self-images and self-esteem.

Encourages and teaches individuals to engage in prayer, fasting, and other spiritual disciplines. May work with evangelists in providing counsel to people and in enabling them in their spiritual maturity.

• *Peace-building Ministry.* Recognizes genuine differences among members in temperament, style, behavior, and beliefs. Labors to help people develop a positive image of each other. Encourages individuals to explore their differences in creative, nonthreatening forums. Fosters the development of positive communication habits, such as clearing up misunderstandings, discouraging rumors, and promoting accurate information and news. Is aware of the larger peace and justice issues in the local community. May have a knowledge of peace and conflict resolution materials for children and adults. Could serve as the local congregational liaison with emerging Temple peace programs and events.

• *Conflict Intercession Ministry.* Deals with more serious interpersonal and group conflicts that emerge, or seem likely to emerge, in the local church. Is accepted in the congregation as a fair and impartial third party who skillfully conducts mediation and other reconciliation methods among the Saints and their friends. May be a minister to those who are involved in or victims of destructive behaviors (for example, adultery, abuse, chemical dependencies). Works to create new ideas and forums that can open dialogue on sensitive issues.

Ministries the Teacher May Be Requested or Elected to Perform

- Serve as recorder of the congregation
- Assist priests and elders as requested
- Teach classes on personal relationships, etc.
- Teach classes on unity and peace

- Serve as member or leader of a teacher's quorum
- Assist in cottage meetings if requested
- If properly trained and gifted, serve as "lay counselor"
- Work in community agencies providing help to the lonely and those needing help in interpersonal relationships
- Provide "friendly greeting" at congregational meetings
- Participate in congregational meetings as requested

Skills to Enhance Aaronic Ministry

Each Aaronic teacher brings to his or her ministry a wide range of abilities and interests. No two teachers are exactly the same. This seems appropriate when one considers the multitude of needs within the church and community. However, to continue to grow in "wisdom and stature," teachers should periodically assess their strengths, weaknesses, and overall effectiveness in ministry. Teachers can enrich their ministerial abilities by taking training classes in communication, reconciliation, and mediation skills. Also, study in spiritual gifts of prayer, fasting, and meditation can increase one's depth of ministry. Finally, it is vital for teachers to ground themselves in the ministry of Jesus and thus constantly be reminded that each person serves others *not* in their own frail ability and incomplete wisdom, but as an extension of love and concern that God has for each person on earth.

Vision for the Future

In a world filled with chaos, destruction, hopelessness, and despair, the promise of God's kingdom brings light, a sense of hope, and the possibility of peace. Among those called to give special ministry through the offering of unique gifts and skills are Aaronic teachers. Called to be peacemakers, to be sensitive to special needs of individuals and families, and to utilize their giftedness in caring and nurture, these ministers are challenged to recognize the worth of all and seek to bring purpose to the essence of life.

The teacher's ministry carries a strong pastoral concern of caring for the body, expressed not only in mediating problems of alienation but more significantly in giving a sensitized, positive, healing ministry that contributes to good interpersonal relationships among the Saints. The need for this ministry is urgent.

The ministry of the teacher is foundational in nature and is concerned with basic life patterns. It is a ministry that supports and strengthens disciples. So vital is this ministry that the church languishes for this power and strength to be unlocked and freed in the congregations of the church.

The role of the teacher is of great relevance for our time. The teacher's work may be a difficult ministry to give. Likewise, it may be a difficult ministry to receive. However, healthy congregational relationships include the fostering of forgiveness, reconciliation, and the transformation of potentially destructive conflicts into constructive opportunities for growth and change. It is a role in the life of the church that requires education, skill, dedication, pastoral care, spiritual maturity, and an awareness of people that penetrates the superficial.

A clarion call is issued to all Aaronic teachers to seek every opportunity to bring reconciliation and healing to those who are bruised, alienated, and floundering. The mediating influence of God's love can be brought to those situations by ministers skilled in peacemaking and reconciliation. May the church endeavor to fully recognize the value of gifted ministers, called and authorized to go to those who are in need. Peace, visibly demonstrated through loving care and concern, is the backdrop of the teacher's ministry. The kingdom will emerge as this hope becomes more evident in the future.

Ruth Ann Wood

Notes

1. Thanks to Galen Worthington for historical research.
2. *True Latter Day Saints Herald* 18, no. 13 (July 1, 1871): 399.
3. Ibid.
4. Ibid., 399–400.
5. Ibid., 401.
6. Josiah Ells, "Duty of a Teacher as a Branch Officer," *True Latter Day Saints' Herald* 19, no. 9 (May 1, 1872): 257.
7. Ibid.
8. "Editorial," *Saints' Herald* 57, no. 34 (August 24, 1910): 821.
9. *Saints' Herald* 60, no. 23 (June 4, 1913): 549.
10. Adapted from Paul M. Edwards, "The Calling of the Teacher," *Studies in Restoration History: The Doctrine and Covenants, Vol. 2* (Independence, Missouri: Herald House, 1988), 10–12.
11. Adapted from "Report of Aaronic Teacher Ministry Committee," *1994 World Conference Bulletin* (April 9, 1994): 235–240.

CHAPTER 7

Being a Priest in Today's Church

I. The Priest as Specialist

Call to Family Ministry

The priest is called to family ministry. Take this sentence to heart. Our people are desperate for a family minister. Our church is desperate for a family minister. Our communities are desperate for a family minister. Be that minister!

From the earliest days of the church, those individuals called to the office of priest have been challenged to be concerned for families. Doctrine and Covenants 17:10b states: "The priest's duty is to…visit the house of each member, and exhort them to pray vocally and in secret, and attend to all family duties."

The importance of family ministry was affirmed in *The Priesthood Manual* of 1934 with the statement, "The basic task of the priest is visiting in the families of the Saints."[1]

A later edition (1949) of the manual amplified the scripture with the comment,

> The phrase "all family duties" includes many things, but perhaps basically could refer to the establishment of sound family life, economically, socially, morally, and spiritually. It might also include encouraging of the fulfillment of family duties to the church…[and] community….[2]

This form of ministry was even extended beyond the families of the church with the 1964 publication of the *Priesthood Orientation Series:*

Home ministry should not be conceived as being solely for the Saints. It is for every home to which the church can extend ministry.[3]

The 1990 edition of *The Priesthood Manual* encourages priesthood to action with the words,

...priesthood members should live close to their people, giving ministry and pastoral care in the full range of life's activities. Therefore, priesthood responsibilities should not be confined to the meetings which take place within the walls of the church building.[4]

If family ministry is so important in the life of the church, why is it so difficult to perform? Why do our priesthood choose to spend their time on other matters? Why is any type of visiting program so hard to implement?

Family ministry needs a champion. It needs someone who will say, "I am a family minister." It needs someone who will say, "The family and its well-being is my concern." It needs someone who will say, "I will spend my time with our families." The priest is called to be that champion.

Dilemma of the Post-Modern Family

The traditional family—husband, wife, and children all living under one roof—is no longer the norm, at least in the United States. In 1992, only 27 percent of American households met the definition of a married couple, husband employed, wife at home, children under age eighteen, living together in the same dwelling.[5]

What is traditional is the nontraditional. As of June 1992, about 24 percent of single women age eighteen to forty-four had borne a child compared to 15 percent a decade earlier. The majority of women with infants are in the work force.

Divorce rates among women in the thirty to forty-four age group are an estimated 40–42 percent. These figures hold across all racial and ethnic groups. The younger the woman at her first marriage, the greater the likelihood she will divorce. Mothers who conceive or bear a child before their first marriage have a greater likelihood of divorce than mothers whose children are conceived after marriage.

Of married women between the ages of fifteen and forty-four with children, 47 percent are in families where both spouses are employed. Women with a college or professional degree are in the work force at a rate more than double that of women with less than four years of high school.

When discussing the changing definition of family, we cannot limit ourselves to describing the young, single-parent mother and her children as the new family. Population statistics also reveal that America is an aging society. The 1990 census found that 12.5 percent of the total population was over age sixty-five. The elderly population increased by more than 20 percent during the 1980s. Nine states had more than one million elderly in 1990; Florida had the largest proportion of people age sixty-five or older: 18 percent.[6]

Two-parent families, single-parent families, blended families, extended families, same-sex families, mixed-race families, couples with no children, couples with adopted children, single people, elderly couples, elderly living alone—how do we tell what is a family today?

Steven Beebe has a definition that appears to fit: "A family unit is made up of any number of persons who live in relationship with one another and are usually, but not always, united by marriage and kinship."[7] This definition is broad and dynamic. It describes a social unit that is in change, and change produces uncertainty.

James Fowler has written insightfully on the normative changes occurring in American society. An increase in life expectancy; greater physical, economic, and social mobility; democratization of education with an attendant rise in critical self-awareness (what constitutes quality and worthiness in life); growing pluralism; and the replacement of the ethic of self-denial with an ethic of self-fulfillment have impacted everyone and every institution, including the family. Not only has the traditional family disappeared, the traditional images of manhood and womanhood have disappeared as well.[8]

These changes have produced uncertainty and ferment that have led many to ask questions about the meaning of their lives, about what they want for themselves and their children. In a study of the religious and spiritual practices of the baby boomers, Wade Clark Roof observes that people are searching for cultural icons that will hold. Cultural icons are the symbols and metaphors that enable individuals to make sense out of life and formulate ways of behaving. The search has led to a reexamination of religious and spiritual themes but in a decidedly free and flexible manner.[9]

Into this arena enter family ministers, who are aware that the family is not as it once was. They are also aware that the nature of religious authority has changed along with everything else. No longer does the pastor receive deferential treatment from the flock. No longer are the pronouncements of the minister accepted without question. What does the family minister do?

Preparation for Family Ministry

An obvious answer to the question is that ministers prepare themselves for family ministry. A degree or college coursework in family counseling would be helpful. Some may choose this option. Others may not be able to pursue formal education and may elect to study the family on their own. Temple School Center has resources that can be helpful, including a course entitled CL 105 Family Ministry. Whatever the choice, the priest needs to increase his or her skills in bringing effective ministry to families.

One way to do this is to be aware that the family is a system. Yes, the family is composed of individuals with their own unique personalities, talents, and interests. But the whole is greater than the sum of its parts.

Virginia Satir, a noted family therapist, likened the family to a mobile: push one member of the family and others are affected. In the family, as in the mobile, all members are in relationship with one another. To change the system or to change a single unit of the system requires an understanding of how the components of the system fit together. It is usually not productive to focus on just one set of relationships in attempting to change the interaction or behavior. The meaning the change has for the entire set of relationships must be examined.[10]

It might also be instructive to think of the congregation as a family. In this analogy, the congregation mirrors the family as a social system. There is a web of relationships that form the structure of the group and influence the way members relate to one another, regardless of the size. Certainly in larger congregations the system is more complex. Nevertheless, the principles that dictate its operation are the same; change in one set of relationships will impact other relationships.

Priests need to be aware that their work with families might also produce change in the congregation. In fact, this may be an objective of the priest's action. There may be relationships in the congregation that need altering, and the best way to bring about this change is to work with families.

Of course, the objective of the priest's ministry may be less specific. It may be more supportive and caring than corrective. It may simply involve encouraging families to participate in the life of the congregation. One must realize that this, too, will impact the group.

In many congregations the web of friendship and kinship ties are very strong. They are sometimes so tightly woven that they prevent new individuals and families from entering. The priest's work may need to be directed to the congregation and to the body's receptiveness to new participants.

From this commentary it should be clear that the ministry the priest is called to bring to families is extensive and requires considerable knowledge and good judgment. Experience and education are probably the best ways to develop the skills necessary to provide this form of ministry. An important part of preparing for ministry to families is determining the message. What does the priest say when he or she goes to meet with families?

Message of Family Ministry

The basic message of family ministry is simple, and it is the same message that underlies all ministry: *God loves you!* That's it. That's what the priest says when he or she visits with people in families.

True, there may be several outcomes that a minister has in mind when initiating ministry in the family context. Achieving these outcomes does require an investment of time and study. Still, the message that instructs the effort is straightforward. The creator of heaven and earth knows who you are and loves you with a love that is unending and unreserved.

Affirmation of one's value is central to the establishment of any positive relationship, within the family or within the church. It is the same with God. People need to hear that they are important to God and that God wants to be present with them. Henri Nouwen writes eloquently of the "trap of self-rejection."

As soon as someone criticizes me, as soon as I am rejected, left alone or abandoned, I find myself thinking: "Well, that proves once again that I am a nobody." Instead of taking a critical look at the circumstances or trying to understand my own and other's limitations, I tend to blame myself—not just for what I did, but for who I am. My negative side says: "I am no good...I deserve to be pushed aside, forgotten, rejected, and abandoned."

Self-rejection is simply seen as the neurotic expression of an insecure person. But neurosis is often the psychic manifestation of a much deeper human darkness: *the darkness of not feeling truly welcome in human existence.* Self-rejection is the greatest enemy of the spiritual life because it contradicts the sacred voice that calls us the "Beloved."[11]

Nouwen continues by stating that we need to recognize and claim the truth of who we are; we are "God's Beloved." The words spoken at Christ's baptism are spoken to us as well,

> ...there is that voice, the voice that speaks from above and from within and that whispers softly or declares loudly: "You are my Beloved, on you my favor rests."[12]

The greatest gift we can give to another is the gift of their belovedness. The priest is called to be the bearer of that gift.

A simple message brought into a complex environment—the message is simple, but not shallow. The environment is complex, but not unnavigable. The simplicity of the message permits the priest to approach his or her task with confidence. It may be all that needs to be said. Then again, it may not.

When working with families, the priest may be confronted with questions that arise from personal uncertainty and spiritual ferment. While the message of God's continuing love undergirds all ministry, people may be searching for evidence of the divine presence and an appropriate response when they feel that presence.

J. W. Fowler maintains that God wants for us what we most want for ourselves. What do I most deeply want? For what do I most deeply yearn? We find our heart's desire by following our deepest longings. When we do, we are seeking answers to questions of meaning, purpose, and identity. Who am I? Why am I here? How am I to live my life? These are questions of vocation. These are questions about our true work.

Our vocation, in Fowler's opinion, is to be God's partner in joint care for creation. Each of us, whether we recognize it or not, have been addressed by God and called into partnership with responsibility for expressing love in our relationships and for working toward peace, justice, and the realization of the full potential of our sisters and brothers in creation. Only by discovering our true vocation will our yearnings be satisfied.[13]

As profound as this thought is, we must be aware that it will not satisfy everyone. Priests need to recognize that they will not have answers to all the questions people ask. This is okay. In fact, it is not the job of the priest to answer people's questions *for* them. Rather, the priest helps people form the questions and encourages them to determine the answers for themselves.

It takes courage to stand in the eye of the soul's storm.[14] This is what the duty of the priest is all about: to stand with the individual or family when the storm is raging and, by doing so, assure them that God is with them as well.

II. The Priest as Generalist

Preaching, Teaching, Expounding, and Exhorting

For years we have been told not to think of priesthood in terms of hierarchy. One priesthood office is not better than another. Individuals are called according to the gifts of God unto them and are to magnify their callings through study and by serving with faith and humility. Good advice.

However, if we truly believe it, why do we still expect the well-educated and financially well-to-do to be elders, high priests, and bishops? If the priest is called to family ministry, then psychiatrists, psychologists, social workers, family therapists, and any social service professional who works with families should be serving as priests. Would we and they be willing to accept this?

Please do not misinterpret these comments. I recognize it is not appropriate for everyone who works with families to be a priest. Many are called to other offices, and rightfully so. The point is that we have not moved very far from the notion of priesthood as hierarchy. It is perhaps more useful to speak of the various priesthood offices as specialties.

The deacon is called to be a specialist in financial management. The elder is called to be a specialist in pastoral ministry. The teacher is called to be a specialist in conflict management. The priest, as I have already advocated, is called to be a specialist in family ministry.

Thinking of priesthood in this way may help reduce the status that may be associated with one office or another. Status is not an issue; competence and special skills are the issues. Individuals called to an office should possess the skills required to minister effectively in that office. If they do not, they should work quickly to acquire them.

In advocating this point of view, I am fully aware that the priest is also called to be a generalist. However, this is not the priest's primary call. Family ministry is the domain of the priest and should receive his or her undivided attention.

What about preaching, teaching, expounding, and exhorting? Yes, the priest may be asked to perform ministerial tasks other than ministering to families. Certainly, these tasks are no less important and should be taken as seriously as family ministry.

Broadening the priest's area of ministerial responsibility demands a broadening of the knowledge base from which the priest works. Our membership has come to expect ministry that is polished and informed. They will accept sincerity but not ignorance. They will be tolerant of imperfection but not slothfulness.

Once again, education is the key. Some may choose to pursue seminary training or an advanced degree in religion as a means of acquiring the knowledge and skills to function effectively as generalists. Others may prefer a self-directed approach to their learning. Temple School Center has a rich curriculum in resources for enhancing one's ministry.

Whatever the choice, it is important that it be made. Our people deserve our very best effort. We cannot put forth this effort by remaining uninformed.

A word about preaching. Do not let it define your ministry. Few would argue that the spoken word is the only means of bringing ministry to people. But what do our actions tell us? In some congregations, little happens in the way of ministry except for the Sunday-morning sermon. This is not to denigrate the ministry of the spoken word, but to put it in its proper place, as *one* form of valid ministry. Spending time with families is of equal or perhaps even greater importance.

Teaching deserves an additional comment as well. You do not teach adults the same way you teach children. Malcolm Knowles, a prominent adult educator, used the word **andragogy** to distinguish the teaching and learning of adults from **pedagogy**, the teaching and learning of children. He also stressed that children's learning is teacher-centered while adult learning is learner-centered. Adults have valuable resources of their own to draw on in their learning—their life experiences. The teacher functions best as a facilitator and resource person.[15] CL900 Guiding Adult Learning is a Temple School Center resource that can assist you in your work with adult learners.

Expounding and exhorting—these are old-fashioned terms dealing with explaining and warning. To expound means to make plain. It involves explaining how the gospel has meaning and can reinvigorate every aspect of life. To exhort means to caution and advise. It implies helping people become aware of the consequences of their actions and attitudes.[16]

These two terms carry a negative connotation. Therefore, great care should be taken in their practice. Loving others, not judging others, is what lies at the heart of ministry. As Nouwen points out in his book *The Return of the Prodigal Son*, the father does not desire to criticize, and neither should we. As parent, God wants only to offer a love that can be freely received and returned. As parent, the only authority God claims is the authority of compassion.

Guilt is not a positive way to motivate people because it relies on feelings of self-rejection. Self-rejection leads us to believe that we are not worthy of God's love. What is clear from the parable is that God is always ready to love and forgive, absolutely independent of our response. God's love does not depend on our repentance, on inner or outer change, on anything. God's love is always there.[17]

Administering the Sacramental Ordinances

In ministering as a generalist, an important task of the priest is to express God's love for people through the administration of the sacramental ordinances of the church.

A sacrament is an oath or pledge of loyalty, a solemn declaration of obedience. An ordinance is an authorized procedure or practice. When combined, they describe an officially sanctioned activity that has the quality of a covenant. A sacramental ordinance implies a binding, a joining of parties in mutual promise and obligation.[18]

The sacramental ordinances provide us with opportunities to share a mutual interchange with God. When entered into with seriousness, we experience God's interest in and commitment to us and, in return, align ourselves with God's purposes for us, the call to vocation. The marker events of our lives are employed as a means to place us before God so that we may be transformed.

Looking at the specific sacramental ordinances, the priest is authorized to officiate in baptism, the Lord's Supper, marriage, and ordination of other members of the Aaronic priesthood. In taking leadership in these symbolic activities, you are speaking and acting for someone else—for the church, for the state, for Christ. As a minister, your presence and action witness of the significance of the event.

III. Summary

In this chapter you have been challenged to be many things: a specialist in family ministry, a champion of the family, a bearer of the gift of God's unrestricted love, an advocate who stands with and for families. You have been encouraged to prepare yourself for ministry both as a specialist and a generalist. You have been reminded that it is okay *not* to have all the answers. You have been urged to see other priesthood members as peers and to allow your ministry to expand beyond preaching. You have also been invited to consider the sacramental ordinances as opportunities for human and divine intention to combine and produce a new unity of purpose.

A final charge: The priest is called to be the carrier of peace to families. We live in a culture of violence. Violence—physical, verbal, and emotional—is legitimized as a way to deal with our problems. Violent confrontations are often not only seen as necessary, but also healthy. The peacemaker, if mentioned at all, is viewed as weak and ineffectual.

Carolyn and David Brock, in their 1994 adult reunion text, *The Gift of Peace*, stress that peacemaking begins at home: the family is the primary peacemaking unit of society. Yet the family is impacted by societal norms and customs. How are our families going to practice peace if what they see around them is violence? How are our families going to learn peace if what they are taught is violence?

The priest is called to bring to families another vision: a vision that peace is possible; a vision that reaches into every area of life with a message of wholeness, dignity, and freedom; a vision that peace is God's desire for the world; a vision that peace is found in a person—Jesus Christ.[19]

Religious congregations are the most important carriers of meaning that we have—with one exception. They are the most important ground of purpose and direction—with one exception. They are the most important source of an essential element of life—human community—with one exception. The exception is the human family.[20]

John W. Noren

Notes

1. *The Priesthood Manual* (Independence, Missouri: Herald House, 1934), 16.
2. *The Priesthood Manual* (Independence, Missouri: Herald House, 1949), 27.
3. A. H. Yale, *Priesthood Orientation Series* (Independence, Missouri: Herald House, 1964), 198.
4. *The Priesthood Manual* (Independence, Missouri: Herald House, 1990), 223.
5. Personal notes, University College Conference, Ohio State University (Columbus, Ohio; March 2, 1992).
6. R. Famighetti, *The World Almanac and Book of Facts 1994* (Mahwah, New Jersey: Funk & Wagnalls, 1993), 957.
7. S. A. Beebe, CL 105 Family Ministry (Independence, Missouri: Temple School Center, 1994), 14.
8. J. W. Fowler, *Becoming Adult, Becoming Christian* (San Francisco: Harper & Row, 1984), 3–11.
9. W. C. Roof, *A Generation of Seekers* (San Francisco: Harper and Row, 1993), 4–5.
10. Beebe, 18.

11. H. J. M. Nouwen, *Life of the Beloved* (New York: Crossroad Publishing Company, 1993), 26–27.
12. Ibid., 26.
13. J. W. Fowler, *Weaving the New Creation* (San Francisco: HarperCollins Publishers, 1991), 120–121.
14. Stan Kimball, "'Come Ye Disconsolate': Is There a Mercy Seat in Mormon Theology?" Plenary Session of the Annual Meeting of the John Whitmer Historical Association, Lamoni, Iowa, (September 24–26, 1993), personal notes.
15 Malcolm Knowles, *The Modern Practice of Adult Education: From Pedagogy to Andragogy* (Chicago: Association Press/Follett, 1980).
16. A. Bruce Lindgren, PA 103 The Priest (Independence, Missouri: Temple School Center, 1994), 7–8.
17. H. J. M. Nouwen, *The Return of the Prodigal Son* (New York: Doubleday, 1992), 75–78.
18. Lyman F. Edwards, CL 115 The Sacraments (Independence, Missouri: Temple School Center, 1987), 6–7.
19. Carolyn Brock and David Brock, *The Gift of Peace* (Independence, Missouri: Herald House, 1993), 13, 43–44.
20. L. B. Mead, *The Once and Future Church: Reinventing the Congregation to a New Mission Frontier* (Washington, D.C.: The Alban Institute, 1991), v.

SECTION III
Spirituality

CHAPTER 8

Drawn to the Stream: Considerations for Personal Spirituality

"As a deer longs for flowing streams, so my soul longs for you, O God." —Psalm 42:1 NRSV

A Lesson from the River

I will never look at rivers the same again.

As I stepped into the cold water of the Michigan stream, I was flanked on both sides by two friends who had taken me there to teach me how to fly fish. (They both have the gift of patience.) As we stepped into the water, I watched them as they began to "read" the river, commenting on its unique contours, noticing the ripples, the pools, and the life above and within the flow of its waters. It was as though the river had a personality and they were attempting to get acquainted. As I spent the afternoon with them, hip-deep in the moving water, I began to appreciate and understand the river as never before. I also began to understand why they spoke of the river so often, both in casual conversation and in moments of serious discussion.

The river is so much like life. In some places, the water flowed fast, as though in a great hurry to get to some important place downstream. In other places, the water slowed down to form deep pools that were of particular interest to the fishermen. The river contained the "stuff" that had been deposited in it far upstream. At the same time, the river was made new with every raindrop that fell or tributary that contributed to it. In the midst of all its various parts though, the river was one continuous flowing "whole."

So it should be in our spiritual lives.

Spirituality is not one compartment of our lives that sits alongside a hundred other compartments. Instead, spirituality has to do with how we integrate all the "parts" of our lives into a unified whole, under the umbrella of our relationship with God. Spirituality is relationships. This not only includes our relationship with God and ourselves, but with family, friends, working associates, neighbors, the church, and the planet on which we live.

There is some danger in defining spirituality in such general terms. Namely, spirituality can be defined so broadly that it could be watered down to mean very little. To avoid this pitfall, an important affirmation should be made. That is, while we are concerned about the myriad parts of life, spirituality is concerned with the possibility of having our life centered in God and then relating to the various aspects of life out of that center. It is what Bernard Cooke refers to as the "reciprocal indwelling"[1] of God's being in us, and our being in God. Continuing with our river analogy, it is the idea that the waters of our lives can be intermingled with both the waters of the Divine and the rivers of human experience.

Some Foundational Thoughts

How we grow in relationship with God is the primary issue of this article. Later on, we will explore several specific ways or paths that can be helpful. Before we consider these however, attention should be given to the following principles which are foundational for a healthy, growing spirituality.

The Focus Is on Relationship

As we consider our desire for spiritual growth, we should remember that the focus of our spiritual journey should be on relationships, and not on a quest for particular spiritual experiences. As we mature, our longing is for an increased awareness of and intimacy with God, the universe, and others. If particular spiritual experiences occur along the way, fine. If not, fine. If particular experiences do occur, we should seek to learn from these experiences, perhaps even cherishing our memory of them. We should not dwell, however, on the experiences or strive after them as a primary object of our concern. In so doing, it is easy for us to develop tunnel vision and become blind to the myriad ways God may relate to us. After all, it should be God whom we are seeking, not a specific type of spiritual expression that we may desire.

An Embrace, Not an Escape

All of us have times when we need to take a break from the frustrations of life. In fact, a healthy spiritual life includes frequent (even daily) times in which we step out of life's rush for a few moments to enter periods of recreating stillness. Unfortunately, there have always been people who have sought to use the guise of "spirituality" as an escape from wrestling with the difficulties of life.

While our spiritual journey should include moments (or even days) of refreshment and retreat, the overall effect of our deepening relationship with God should be to help us embrace life in its fullness. If we are in the process of becoming Christlike, then what was Christ like? Even a casual review of the Gospels reveals that Christ did not model a spirituality that called for complete escape from human experience. Jesus ate, drank, wept, sweat, embraced, went to parties, had friends, felt pain, experienced betrayal, got dirty, celebrated, and experienced countless other human experiences, including death. Although he spoke of a kingdom, he never advocated an escape from this world. Quite the contrary; after the resurrection, he specifically sent his disciples into the world (see Matthew 28) and continues to do so (see Doctrine and Covenants 153:9).

If our discipleship involves the immersion of our lives into the human condition to help transform the kingdoms of this world into the kingdom of God, then our spiritual journey will include a full embrace of both joy and suffering, fellowship and loneliness, laughter and tears. The point is: life can be experienced within the context of our relationship with God and can be meaningful subject matter in our prayers and meditations.

Honor the Cycles of Spiritual Living

There are times when we may sense a great closeness with the Divine, as though we were on the mountaintop with God. There are other times when we may feel as though God is absent or "on leave" and we are in the valleys of despair and isolation. Most of the time, we live on the hills and plateaus somewhere in between. While it is true that we can do—or fail to do—a number of things that affect the way we feel about our relationship with God, it is also true that there are "cycles" in our spiritual journey that do not always coincide neatly with how "good" we have been or how diligently we have been engaged in spiritual discipline (although such things certainly do have a profound effect on our lives). Spiritual maturing has to do with acknowledging and living faithfully in all these cycles, instead of always seeking the good times or the mountaintop. If we are always seeking the mountaintop, how will we learn the lessons of the desert?* The point is to continue faithfully and prayerfully in each cycle of the spiritual journey. The question is one of attentiveness: "What am I learning in this stage of my journey?"

Each One's Path Is Unique

I remember a game played at a church camp one summer that involved a relay race. People of all ages participated in the race which, at one point, involved reaching into a pile of clothing and putting on whatever outfit you happened to grab over the top of the clothes you already had on. Participants then finished the race while wearing the ill-fitting apparel. Obviously, some people ended up racing with clothing they could hardly squeeze into, while others were racing with oversized clothes that kept falling down. All in all, it was a hilarious sight.

Sometimes we approach spirituality the same way. We do so whenever we attempt to wear someone else's "spiritual clothing." It is easy to fall into the trap of thinking that to be truly "spiritual," we need to think like, live like, or have experiences like some other person.

Certainly there are important principles, priorities,

---

* The "desert" has long been a metaphor to describe the experience of feeling spiritually dry and apart from God (and thus, not due to any particular sinfulness or lack of faith). In the desert, we are left to confront ourselves and can therefore learn a great deal about how we think, how we feel, and what motivates us. Although not particularly pleasant, it can be a valuable time in our spiritual journey.

and practices that many of us will have in common (such as the centrality of God, our need for love, and the discipline of prayer, to name just a few). Still, we need to honor the uniqueness of each person and consequently the uniqueness of their own spiritual journey. This is not to say that "anything goes" as long as a person is following his or her personal path. (Heaven only knows that some paths have led to wholesale catastrophe and tragedy.) It is to affirm that as individuals we relate to God in different ways and that we need not be concerned about forcing our way on others. Neither should we be worried about imitating someone else's approach to spirituality.

The foregoing does not mean that we should not learn from one another. We should take every opportunity to do so. Sharing insights and experiences, and learning new approaches to prayer, meditation, and other spiritual disciplines is a vital part of spiritual growth. But as we learn from one another, we can do so without falling into the trap of believing that our spiritual journey (or spiritual experiences) should be cast in the same mold as someone else's. To do so would be to deny our own uniqueness.

Individuals experience God differently. A healthy spirituality affirms that God can be experienced through the intellect, the emotions, creation, art, music, and the body, to name just a few ways. Some persons find it easy to connect with God in the quiet of a mountain forest, whereas others feel the pulse of the divine heartbeat in the energy of a busy city. There is no one way to experience God.

Fortunately, growing in relationship with God includes sharing common blessings and struggles with others, as well as discovering and honoring the uniqueness of our own journey.

Earlier it was mentioned that the purpose of this article is to address how we can grow in our relationship with God. Obviously, no article, book, or library of books can recount all the important responses to this matter. Consequently I will not attempt to cover a broad base of disciplines and ministries that can be incorporated into our spiritual journey (such things as study and fasting, for example, will not be addressed here). I would, however, like to present four particular paths or ways we can travel that can be helpful, if not central, in a growing relationship with God: meditation, prayer, companionship, and service.

The Path of Meditation

When groups of people are asked, "What images come to mind when you hear the word meditation?" a variety of responses are usually offered. Typically these responses range from such images as "quiet contemplation" to that of bearded gurus sitting atop some distant mountain sharing enlightenment with spiritual pilgrims. In the midst of these many images, meditation exists as a long-standing and rich spiritual discipline in the Christian tradition, as well as in all of the world's great religions. When cultivated as a personal discipline, meditation can be a profound means of deepening one's awareness of the presence of God.

The Purpose of Meditation

We are children of our own culture. In many ways, this is a blessing, because culture offers its members a rich tapestry of enriching traditions and symbols. At the same time we may also carry some unnecessary baggage in the course of our living in a certain time and place. William

Countryman reminds us that "Christians are repeatedly tempted to settle in with the culture of their day and place. They assume protective coloration....They turn into guardians of the public mores...."[2]

For twentieth-century Westerners, some of the baggage we carry is found in our living in a "hurry up" society in which life becomes frantic with a thousand voices competing for a portion of our time and attention. Consequently, our minds are often cluttered with an avalanche of concerns racing through our consciousness at once. We have a great need for calm, quiet, and an internal peace from which we may engage in life's adventure. Intellectually we may understand that God is always present, but that is not the problem.

> The problem is that we lose awareness of God's presence, and often when we most need it. For all practical purposes we can become practicing atheists at such times. In meditating on a daily basis, we are devoting a specific time to being conscious of the presence of God so that we are more likely to retain this awareness at other times.[3]

Meditation is a discipline that helps us to live out the admonition of the psalmist to "Be still, and know that I am God" (Psalm 46:10). The purpose of meditation is to quiet the body and the mind in order to be more attentive to God's presence, as well as to increase our awareness of our whole self and our environment. Later in this chapter, several meditation exercises will be presented, but there are some basic considerations that should be taken into account first.

A Special Time and Place

While meditation can, in some form, be practiced virtually anywhere and anytime, there is much to be said about establishing a particular time and place for this discipline in order to nurture an environment of stillness and peace. Although the "right time" for daily meditation varies from person to person, the important thing is to select a time of day when you can be by yourself and not be rushed. The length of time devoted to this discipline will also vary, but allowing fifteen to twenty minutes is often a reasonable time frame to begin with.

The location of your meditation practice is also an important consideration. Here again, personal preferences must be honored, but it is important that the place of meditation (at least at first) be quiet and aesthetically and physically comfortable, as well as being a place where you are unlikely to be disturbed. (You may have to be creative, or even do some family "contracting" to find such a time and place.)

Relaxation

Before presenting specific meditation exercises, a word should be said about the discipline of relaxation. In our "hurry up" world, it is so easy to bring the frantic scatteredness of the day into our time of prayer and meditation. Consequently, we may pray often yet neglect the necessary discipline of "quieting" our lives to "be still" in the presence of God. This becomes especially significant when we are reminded of the intimacy between the body, mind, and spirit—if one of these is under stress, our whole self is affected.

With this in mind, we should be reminded of the benefits of taking a few moments to relax before engaging in specific exercises of meditation or prayer. One way to do this is to begin by sitting or lying in a comfortable position and simply becoming aware of your feet and ankles. Are they harboring any stress or tension? If so, you can relax them, releasing any tension that may be there, and imagining your feet and ankles to be calm, limp, warm, relaxed. You can proceed by slowly going up your body, checking each area for any hidden stress, and then becoming aware of what it feels like to relax that part of the body, causing it to be calm and at peace. After you have taken several minutes to move from your feet up to your face and head, relaxing each area as you go, become aware of your breathing.

With every breath, you can imagine that you are breathing out any residual stress that may be within you, while you inhale the pure peace of God. After several breaths, you can imagine that both your inhaling and your exhaling are filled with peace as you let the rhythm of your breathing deepen your relaxation.

Many times we do not understand how tense we are until we intentionally relax. While this may cause some people to feel sleepy at first, this process of relaxation, especially when coupled with other prayer/meditation exercises, can help us develop minds that are more alert and free from unneeded stress.

Specific Exercises

After taking the time to relax, there are a number of specific meditation exercises you can engage in. Within the Christian tradition alone, there are countless meditation styles and exercises, and no single meditation will be "just right" for every person.

Consequently, you need to pick and choose which meditations may be best at this point in your life. One way to do this is to try a particular meditation each day for thirty days. At the end of this time, you should have a feel for whether this particular exercise is helpful. Reading widely in this field will help you be aware of many different meditation styles and exercises. There is only space here though, to present four specific exercises: meditation on scripture, on breathing, on creation, and on "centering" in Christ.

Meditation on Scripture

One of the classic meditations in the Christian tradition is meditation on scripture. While this has been done a number of ways, two are examined here.

One way of meditating on scripture is to select a scriptural story and enter into it, experiencing it with all your senses. To do this, begin by selecting a scriptural text. After reading it a couple of times, put the scriptures down, close your eyes, and relax in the manner described above.

After focusing attention on your breathing for a few minutes and as you begin to feel sufficiently calm, call into your consciousness the scriptural story. Play out the scriptural story on a great movie screen in your mind. In this meditation, though, do not simply sit back and watch the movie. Instead imagine that you rise up from your chair and "enter" the scene, experiencing the unfolding story as one who is there. As the story unfolds, what do you see? What do you hear or smell or feel? Without manipulating or hurrying the story, allow it to unfold around you. After the story is finished, continue to sit quietly, allowing the gentle rhythm of your breathing to keep you calm and focused. As you sit, consider what words, images, or feelings from the scriptural story stand out to you. How is God present in the story? After several minutes of this, you may wish to return attention to your breathing for a few minutes, allowing yourself to conclude your meditation in a calm, focused manner.

A second type of scriptural meditation is the meditation on a scriptural phrase. In this meditative experience, a brief scriptural phrase is repeated silently as you breathe. For example, suppose you were to focus on the scripture "Love your neighbor as yourself" (Mark 12:31 NRSV). After a few moments of relaxation, begin to repeat this phrase in harmony with your breathing. As you inhale, allow the words "love your neighbor" to fill your consciousness. As you exhale, the words "as yourself" can occupy your awareness. Continue in this manner for several minutes, repeating the phrase, "Love your neighbor as yourself," in harmony with each breathing cycle. After ten to fifteen minutes, you may wish to conclude this portion of your meditation and just sit quietly for a while. Perhaps thoughts about the scripture will arise or you will just want to sit and enjoy a time of peace and calm.

The purpose of this meditation is to allow a single scriptural phrase to sink deeply into your consciousness. Consequently, it is not the intent here to analyze this scripture, although analysis should have an important place in the life of the church and can enrich meditation. Instead, it is the intent of this meditation simply to allow the scripture to enter your awareness and speak in whatever way it may at that particular time in your life.

If you are considering this type of meditation, please keep two things in mind. First, it is a good idea to select a relatively brief scriptural phrase. Second, the words you repeat should be in harmony with your breathing, as opposed to modifying your breathing to somehow match the rhythm of the phrase you are repeating.

Meditation on Breathing

In all the great religious traditions where meditation has played an important part, special attention has been given to breathing. For many people, focusing attention on their breathing in meditation is a helpful means of tuning out distractions. Some Christians who practice "meditation on breathing" like to do so while being aware of God's Spirit as the life-giving "breath" that connects us to all creation and ultimately to God. You may wish to try the following meditation.

After assuming a comfortable position and sitting (or lying) quietly for a few moments, close your eyes, and take a deep "cleansing" breath. Now, with your next breath, begin counting your exhalations. The object here is to have your whole being involved in the counting. The entire focus of your mind should be on each breath and on counting "one," "two," "three," etc. Some people have suggested it is better to count up to four or five breaths and then start over, repeating this cycle several times, rather than counting sequentially as high as you can go.

As you continue, you will discover that your mind will wander repeatedly. Do not be disappointed or upset, but simply return your attention gently to breathing and counting. As you experience this meditation, be aware of God's Spirit as the divine breath that connects you to both creation and Creator. After about ten to fifteen minutes of this, you may open your eyes and conclude your meditation.

Meditation on Creation

For many people an interior spirit of peace and a sense of God's presence is often experienced when they are close to nature. For contemporary urban people in particular, it is so easy to separate ourselves from the beauty, simplicity, and rejuvenating essence of creation. Many of us lead fast-paced, busy lives in which we bounce back and forth between home, office, restaurants, meeting rooms, etc. Insulated in our cars, we travel from place to place, frequently too preoccupied with our busy schedules to appreciate (or even notice) the greenness of the grass, the intricately simple splendor of a tree, or the majesty of approaching rain clouds. We are quick to call God "Creator," yet amazingly hesitant to slow down long enough to bask in the creation. Gerald May does well to remind us:

> We are marvelously incarnated creations, but around us there exists a whole universe of other marvelous creations, of space, form, and energy. At the root of *all* of this is the Creator. We may be very specially loved in God's heart, but we are not alone there.[4]

Meditation on some element of nature can be a meaningful way to rediscover the wonder of the universe and to be reminded of God's ever-present being. One way to engage in this type of meditation is to select some object of nature that is beautiful or fascinating to you. This could be a plant, tree, rock, body of water, or the sky. After identifying the object of your meditation, sit or lie quietly for a few minutes, allowing your breathing to relax you. As you begin to feel calm, focus your attention on the chosen object . Your task is not to analyze or to "think hard" about the object. Rather you are simply to sit and enjoy it, appreciating its color, texture, and its various features. Simply slow down and enjoy the gift of this one small portion of creation, allowing your mind to consider the Creator.

Another form of this type of meditation is the nature walk. In the nature walk meditation, we are not just walking in the woods (or wherever) while we pray or think about something else. We are walking in the woods to clear our minds of distractions and notice the beauty of the woods itself—its trees, wildlife, etc. Here again, the purpose is to take time to enjoy the blessings of creation and, in so doing, have our awareness drawn to the Creator. We are not talking about some sophisticated pantheism here, but the appreciation of life, beauty, and its author. This form of meditation can be practiced on the beach, in the mountains, or in any crowded city or neighborhood street where there is sky overhead or growing things to ponder.

A "Centering" in Christ Meditation[5]

Many people have found the following meditation to be helpful. It can help clear our hearts and minds from distraction while we "center" our attention on Christ. To prepare for this meditation, sit quietly for a few moments, enjoying the stillness. You may want to close your eyes, or you may want to look at something that tends to calm your spirit and draw your attention to Christ (a beautiful picture, a tree in your backyard). After several moments of sitting quietly, you may continue as follows:

Begin by resting your hands on your lap with the palms turned downward in a symbolic expression of "letting go." As you do, allow yourself to become aware of anything that may be causing you to feel disturbed, upset, or estranged from God. As these things arise in your mind, you may inwardly say something like, "Lord, I release the anger I feel toward Bill. I relinquish the fear I have about my dentist appointment today. I surrender my frustration about the problem I seem to be having with Mary." Whatever it is that weighs you down or concerns you, release it "palms down."

After you sense that you are finished "releasing," turn your palms upward in an expression of receiving. This time, fill the voids made when you released your concerns. For example, with your palms now up, you might inwardly say, "Lord, I want to receive your love for Bill.

I receive the spirit of peace for my dentist appointment...the gift of forgiveness for Mary."

After you have finished this period of "palms up," spend the rest of your meditation time in silence. During this time, do not be concerned about praying *for* or *about* anything. Simply focus your attention on Christ, inwardly satisfied to simply be present in this moment of quiet worship.

Dealing with Distraction

Before leaving this discussion of meditation, a word must be shared about dealing with distractions, which are a major issue for most people who attempt to make meditation a part of their spiritual life. There are two kinds of distractions in meditation. The first kind is **external distraction** and includes such things as the telephone and other interruptions. These may be troublesome but can be dealt with by securing the right time and space for your meditations.

Even more troublesome, though, and more difficult to dispel, are **internal distractions.** These are the distractions that come from our own minds when we begin to be still and relax. As we do, it is often the case that we will be flooded with a myriad of distracting thoughts. It is as though the mind is saying, "Now that you've slowed down, let me dump into your consciousness every little thought you've been too busy to hear." How frustrating it is to sit down to meditate, only to have our own minds remind us of the laundry that needs doing, errands that need running, and a host of other things that need attention.

When this happens, the worst thing we can do is to launch a frontal assault and attempt to push the distraction out of our minds. When we do this, we only give it more power. It is much more effective simply to acknowledge the distraction, let it pass through your mind, and affirm that you can care for it later if you choose. When internal distractions come, do not become irritated; simply let them pass, because learning how to deal with them is a part of your spiritual journey. The following counsel from Jack Kornfield is well-heeded advice.

> When we first undertake the art of meditation, it is indeed frustrating. Inevitably, as our mind wanders and our body feels the tension it has accumulated and the speed to which it is addicted, we often see how little inner discipline, patience, or compassion we actually have. It doesn't take much time with a spiritual task to see how scattered and unsteady our attention remains even when we try to direct and focus it....
>
> The essence of this connecting [of our mind, body, and heart] is the bringing back of our attention again and again to the practice we have chosen. Prayer, meditation, repeating sacred phrases, or visualization gives us a systematic way to focus and steady our concentration.[6]

If a distracting thought takes you away from your meditation, do not become angry but simply return your attention to your meditation. In all likelihood you will need to do this again, and again, and again. Meditation, like all disciplines, is a practice that takes a lifetime to learn. We should, therefore, not be discouraged if we are easily distracted at first. It is better to just continue in your meditation practice, learning as you go.

The Path of Prayer

Several years ago, I was listening to a conversation between two people who were discussing their ideas about prayer. One of them, who seemed to have a desire to teach the other, began to expound his understanding of the nature of prayer. "The key to prayer", he said, "is to have a clear idea of what it is that you want, and then search the scriptures until you find out how to pray and what to do in order to get it." I listened as this well-meaning person then produced a piece of paper listing a number of "wants." The list included such things as wealth, a nice house, personal peace, and a loving wife, and next to each item on the list was a proposed formula that told him which scriptures to read and how to pray to obtain the things he desired.

As I continued to listen to this person's explanation of how prayer works, I thought to myself, how sad. The prayer life he was describing was not a prayer life that embraced having a *relationship* with God. Instead, this person was promoting a mechanistic prayer life in which God appeared to be little more than a great computer, who would produce a desired output only if the proper input was given.

The purpose of prayer is not to treat God as though God were a resource for personal fulfillment. In its highest form, prayer is not primarily concerned with the receiving of particular blessings (although this certainly has an important place). Rather the primary concern of prayer is our *relationship* with God. Prayer is the arena in which we praise, laugh, cry, petition, and wrestle with life's issues. This is not done, however, in a cause-and-effect mode with some great cosmic machine. Prayer is the language that is experienced in our relationship with the living God. It is a language that is verbal, nonverbal, written, painted, danced, acted out, wept, laughed, and given expression in countless other ways. Like all languages, prayer is as concerned with listening as it is with speaking.

The question then arises, "How do we pray?" Many of us have grown up being exposed to only one prayer style. For most of us this is a way of praying in which we form words in our minds and then express them to God either vocally or silently. This is the type of prayer we hear most often at church and may be most accustomed to in our personal lives.

This "traditional" way of praying is certainly a time-honored, legitimate, and meaningful prayer style. It is not, however, the only way to pray. With this in mind, let's take a brief look at four other ways of praying. We will do so, not because any of these ways is superior to another, but because learning to pray in different modes can enrich the tapestry of our prayer life, and therefore our relationship with God.

The Personal Prayer Journal

One creative and insightful way to engage in prayer is to do so with a personal prayer journal, in which a person writes his or her prayers in the form of a letter. This can be helpful in at least two ways.

First, while it is true that there are similarities between our verbal patterns of expression and our written thoughts, it also appears to be true that some feelings, thoughts, and insights are expressed differently when we write them as opposed to when we simply say them. It is as though speaking and writing access different parts of our creative mind, and consequently the act of writing our prayers can be a significant mode of expression and insight.

Second, the act of keeping our prayers in a journal allows us to go back from time to time and review what we have been praying about. We have a tendency, perhaps, to view moments of insight and meaningful prayer as individual experiences. When we review our prayer journal, however, it is sometimes possible to see larger patterns of insight emerge that may not be readily discernable to us when we view our prayers only as separate experiences. Keeping such a journal may help us appreciate the principle affirmed in Isaiah's testimony that God will teach us "line upon line; here a little, and there a little" (Isaiah 28:10).

I remember, in reviewing my journal one day, looking back over about three months' worth of entries. I was surprised to discover the number of times in which the word *peace* was used. In taking a closer look, I was even more surprised to see the context in which I was using the word. Without going into the details of the experience, I will just say that the way that I was using the word *peace* revealed an area of self-centeredness in my life that I was not previously aware of but was now able to perceive and address.

If you are interested in experimenting with this approach to prayer, you may want to try the following:

Select a specific time and place for your prayers where you can go each day for ten to fifteen uninterrupted minutes. Take a pen and notebook with you. In the top corner of the first page of the notebook, write the date. Now, begin to compose your letter to God, writing whatever it is that you wish to express in your prayer-writing. Some days, you may feel inclined to write a great deal. Other days, you may feel like writing only a sentence or two, spending the rest of your prayer time in quiet contemplation. In any event, try this for thirty days. Then go back and review your journal, looking for any patterns of thought or insights that may emerge.

If you find this particular prayer style to be helpful, you may want to continue with it, although it is probably not necessary to review your journal each month. Reviewing your prayer entries once every three months or so should be sufficient. (It is also good advice not to be too concerned with reading your past prayers until it's time for your quarterly journal review.)

A Prayer in the Evening

The following is a wonderful way to pray based on an exercise presented by Ben Campbell Johnson.[7] To engage in this exercise, allow fifteen minutes or so in the evening to go over your day. First of all, take a few moments to be still and to calm yourself. Next, prayerfully review the events of your day, beginning with what you did immediately after awakening, and proceeding until evening. What did you do today? What did you think or feel? Do you perceive any brokenness in your day? Are there reasons to be grateful? Without becoming obsessed or putting yourself down, do you perceive sins that you need to confess? Are there people for whom you need to pray?

Gradually go over your day, prayerfully considering these questions. Do not rush or be harsh with yourself. Instead, gently hold the day in your awareness, understanding that as you consider the day in this fashion, it is possible for you to perceive how God was present, perhaps in ways you had not realized.

A Prayer by the Ocean

In recent years I have discovered that a number of people have enjoyed the following prayer exercise which involves use of the imagination.

Begin by sitting or lying quietly, closing your eyes, and going through the relaxation process described earlier in this article. After a few minutes of focusing attention on your breathing, imagine yourself walking along a beach by a beautiful stretch of ocean. As you walk, see the sights of water, sky, and sand; be aware of their colors. Hear the sounds of the surf, feel the gentle offshore breeze, and inhale the subtle smells of salt and sea. When you feel ready, imagine yourself sitting down on the sand. Specifically, sit down on that part of the beach where the white foam of the waves rolls up to you and barely caresses the sand right in front of you. Sit there for several moments, allowing the rhythm of the surf and the beauty of the moment to bring you to new levels of relaxation, attentiveness, and peace.

After a while, imagine that you look up and see Christ standing in the surf, about waist-deep in the water. Recognize that he wants to share time with you.

Now, allow whatever it is that you want to share with Christ to rise into your consciousness. This may be a thought, a feeling, a word of praise, a desire, or simply the affirmation that you are glad to be present here in this moment. Whatever it is, place what you want to share on the outgoing wave, and watch as the wave carries it out to Christ. Now watch as Christ places something for you on the next incoming wave, which then rolls up onto the beach, carrying Christ's gift to you.

In this manner, continue to share your thoughts and feelings with Christ, placing them on the outgoing wave and receiving back the gifts Christ would send you. For several minutes you can do this, experiencing the waves in various ways. Some may gently roll in, their white foam barely kissing the sand in front of you. Others may thunder their way in, hitting you chest-high and sending you rolling backward in a delightful expression of celebration and acceptance.

When you feel as though this prayer time has reached an end, imagine that you stand and walk back down the beach. When you are ready, open your eyes.

No prayer style is for everyone, but for many people who find meaning in using their imagination, this can be a delightful way of engaging in prayer.

An Incarnational Prayer[8]

This prayer style attempts to include your whole self in prayer. It is called "incarnational" because in this exercise your prayer is a movement that proceeds (metaphorically) from various parts of your body, as you pray with your lips, eyes, ears, feet, and hands. You may want to experiment with the following:

In the morning, after a few minutes of becoming quiet and still, begin to pray with your lips. What is it you need to say to God as you begin your day?

You may then want to pray with your eyes, where you are not concerned with words but with pictures and images. For example, if you are praying for two friends having marital trouble, you may wish to close your eyes and picture the two of them standing in a room with a brick wall between them. In your picture you may see Christ enter the room and encourage them to tear down the wall gradually. Watch them as they remove the wall, brick by brick, and then embrace one another. Present this image to God as your prayer.

Next, you can consider the role of your ears, because prayer is as much about listening as it is speaking. As you look ahead into the new day, can you be open to hearing the sound of God's presence both in the quiet places of the early morning as well as in the rush of traffic at noon? Perhaps God's whisper will come to you in the utterance of a skilled preacher, or perhaps in the unintended wisdom of a child at play. It may be that today you will be confronted by the Divine in the reading of scripture, or such confrontation may occur as you are watching the evening news. How will you pray with your ears today?

As you stand at the threshold of a new day, how will you pray with your feet? Think about where you will walk today. Give consideration to the places you will go, to the environments you will be in, to the people you will be with. It has been said often about life in the church that "people vote with their feet," which is to say that our feet will take us to the places we value and will avoid places that bear little relevance for us. The suggestion here is that the very act of going somewhere can be experienced as an expression of prayer. It is as if we are saying, "Where do I go today in my desire to follow Christ?" When thought of in this light, is not my walking to volunteer at the soup kitchen an act of prayer? If you know that a colleague at work needs a caring, listening ear, it is possible to experience every footstep that you take down the hallway to his or her office as one nonverbal word after another in a sentence of unspoken prayer.

Finally, consider the matter of how you can pray with your hands. This is what some people have called "doing prayer." I remember a time several years ago when our community was threatened by flooding after several days of torrential rain. People throughout the community, including myself, were praying for those citizens living in the low-lying areas of town. At a certain point, though, our prayers did not seem complete until we actually left our homes, went down to the threatened part of town, and helped fill and place the thousands of sandbags that needed to be set up. In that moment, the act of carrying bags of sand was not something "other than" prayer. The work done that afternoon felt more like an extension of prayer itself. What portion of your praying can you extend with your hands today?

As we learn to pray with our lips, eyes, ears, feet, hands, heart, and mind, we are reminded that we need not compartmentalize prayer into some tiny corner of our lives. Prayer can be something that involves our entire self.

The Path of Companionship

One often-quoted story in scripture is about Jesus' appearance to the disciples walking on the road to Emmaus (see Luke 24:12–35). A significant aspect of the story is that Jesus was found in fellowship with these two disciples as they traveled and talked *together*. Herein lies an important principle of growing in relationship with God: it is a shared journey. While there are some dimensions of our spiritual living that must be experienced in solitude or as personal struggle, it is also true that life in Christ calls us to know the companionship of other pilgrims and friends along the way. Thomas Moore suggests that, "If the body is in pain, one of the first things to look for is infection; if the soul is in pain, we might look for lack of friendship."[9]

During our life's journey we will have relationships with a great number of people. Some will be affirming, while others will be negative. Some will strengthen us, while others will drain us. Some will be superficial, while others may be characterized by great depth. What I want to describe next is one type of relationship that, if nurtured, can be of tremendous help to us in our spiritual growing.

Several years ago I approached three friends and shared with them a particular desire I had in my life. That desire was to identify two or three people who might be willing to be intentional about supporting one another in our spiritual journeys. I suggested it might be worth the effort to get together from time to time just to open our lives to one another for sharing, support, and exploration into some of life's pertinent issues. All three friends echoed this same desire in their lives, and we agreed to get together.

We met approximately once every two months or so, and as we did, something valuable happened. We typically would begin our gatherings with joking and laughter, because we were honestly delighted just to be together. After a few minutes, though, one of us would begin to help the group "shift gears" by asking some simple question such as, "Well, how is everyone doing?" At this point, the fun and laughter of our fellowship would not diminish, but the *tone* of our gathering and the focus of our attention would shift as we began to share with each other. One by one, we would share about how we were doing in our lives. We spoke of hopes and joys, as well as disappointments and hurts. We shared our faith as well as our doubts. We explored ways of prayer and meditation and spoke candidly of the God whom we all loved, but who was so often a mystery to us. We talked about the church, our families, and our society, and although we were in very different places theologically and politically, it was all right. We shared ideas, questioned one another, and did a lot of listening as we supported each other in our spiritual journeys.

We met together for seven years, and it remains one of the greatest helps in my journey that I have ever known. It is not so much that we did anything friends would not ordinarily do with each other, but we did make a covenant to be *intentional* about the way we supported one another. In recent years, I have met with other groups of friends in a similar manner and have been reminded of the value of such relationships. I have also been a bit surprised to discover the large number of people—especially men—who have never been in such a relationship. Even more common appears to be the experience of people who have friends to share with, but who only experience deep personal sharing when it occurs in unplanned, serendipitous moments.

Spirituality is concerned with how all the parts of our lives can be integrated into a unified whole, under the umbrella of our relationship with God. The very notion that we can "figure life out" on our own is ludicrous and leaves us vulnerable to the awful trap of being exposed to only our own interpretation of things. Finding companionship in our spiritual journey is essential. For some, there may be no felt need for the intentional kind of meeting together described above. For others, though, such gatherings may be a much desired experience. It is for this latter group that the following three suggestions are offered.

First, be concerned with identifying a relatively small number of friends to meet with, perhaps between one and four. Groups larger than this will tend to become overly formal. Friends invited to this "Emmaus fellowship" should be people who would be comfortable sharing with one another and who will honor the principle of confidentiality. They may or may not be members of the RLDS Church.

Second, you should move heaven and earth to make sure that the group experience does *not* become programmed. While there is certainly great value in structured support groups, the group intended here is not a class, a study group, or a formal part of congregational program. Neither is it to be a forum for disgruntled individuals to talk about how things "ought to be." *It is simply a group of friends getting together to support one another in their spiritual journeys.*

Third, do not worry about "getting serious," as though spiritual support means having to put on our "poker faces" as we now turn our attention to other-worldly affairs. It is much better simply to be yourselves as you talk together about your spiritual concerns. Likewise, do not *attempt* to be deep. Depth of sharing will come naturally as trust builds and needs arise. Forcing what may appear to be deeper sharing will only keep things superficial. Listen to each other. Talk about the "stuff" of your lives and your relationships with God. Laugh together and have fun! If necessary, cry together. Let the needs of your lives and the places in your journeys determine the content and tone of your being together. Care deeply for one another. "In friendship there may be more not-doing than doing. Friendship doesn't ask for a great deal of activity, but it does require loyalty and presence."[10]

The Path of Service

From time to time, I hear people say something like, "We've got to get our act together spiritually, and then we can reach out to other people." I appreciate a portion of the idea expressed here that suggests that we need to be caring for our own spiritual house to be able to help others. I heartily disagree, though, with the assumption that outreach and service are somehow secondary concerns, to be undertaken only after we get our "spiritual" act together. I would even go so far as to say that without service to others, our spirituality will be grossly stagnated or will result in a personal piety no longer relevant to human need. In the words of Dutch theologian Edward Schillebeeckx, "A decision of faith which does not find any point of contact in human experience is irrational...."[11]

While it is true that God is to be found in the quiet places of meditation and prayer, it is also true that God is to be found in the turmoil of human struggle. If we do not attempt to meet God in both places, our discipleship will be out of balance. We will also be cheating others and ourselves out of the blessing that comes when we cast our lives headlong into the muck and mire of the world, only to find God there waiting for us.

In this regard, there are countless things we can do. This is so much the case that the immensity of human need around us may at times be overwhelming. There are so many good programs, so many places where we are needed. Consequently, the question arises, "Where do I begin?"

There is not room in this article, or in a hundred articles, to address the countless ways we can serve. There are two questions we *can* ask ourselves here that may be helpful, however.

First of all, what is your personal mission? Out of the many things you could possibly do, where do you feel called? What gifts do you have? What skills do you need to develop through education, training, and experience to be more effective? These are not questions to be answered quickly, but ones that call for prayerful consideration as we consider the needs in our world. Identifying your personal mission does not assume that you close your eyes and ears to issues that fall outside your specific missional concern. It does, however, help you focus your energy and personal resources toward that area of service for which you may have the greatest passion. Some people may feel called to enter the political arena, while others may be concerned with local housing projects, the environment, caring for children and families, the elderly, the hungry, or a great many other things.

Working to identify your personal mission and crafting a personal mission statement can be a deeply spiritual thing if you sincerely work at it, review it, and attempt to live it out. "[I]t forces you to think through your priorities deeply, carefully, and to align your behavior with your beliefs."[12] No person is called to do everything, but what is your mission?

A second question: Who needs you? Sometimes we think of grand acts of service we can render that relate to global issues, when right under our noses we may have a spouse who is frustrated because no one is helping with the dishes. The way of service may draw us into larger issues of community or even global concern, but it should also include attention to the mundane, routine chores of life. We should not neglect the social issues of our day, but neither should we neglect the child in our midst who needs help tying their shoes.

In the scriptures, Jesus was forever found with people in need. If we are to grow in our relationship with God, this is where we shall be found as well.

A Return to the River

I began this article with a story about being in a river. I learned a lot and was reminded of much that day.

During my time in the river, I learned how to get my line out when it was snagged in the brush. I learned how to wade into the fast water and how to pay attention to the deep, quiet pools. I learned (again) what it was like to make countless mistakes while trying over and over to get it right. I was reminded of the importance of friends, the value of quiet, and the goodness of ultimately going back into the world. (I also caught a fish!)

As we consider our personal spiritual lives, may we remember that God—*our living water*—is to be encountered in the quiet place of meditation and prayer, in the leadership of the Spirit, in the companionship of friends, family, and others along the way, and in the midst of human turmoil and need.

To these streams, let us be drawn.

David D. Schaal

Notes

1. Bernard J. Cooke, *The Distancing of God: The Ambiguity of Symbol in History and Theology* (Minneapolis, Minnesota: Fortress Press, 1990), 6.
2. L. William Countryman, *Good News of Jesus: Reintroducing the Gospel* (Valley Forge, Pennsylvania: Trinity Press International, 1993), 11.
3. William E. Hulme, *Celebrating God's Presence* (Minneapolis, Minnesota: Augsburg, 1988), 25.
4. Gerald G. May, *Care of Mind, Care of Spirit: Psychiatric Dimensions of Spiritual Direction* (San Francisco: Harper & Row, 1982), 45.
5. Based on a meditation exercise written by Richard J. Foster in *Celebration of Discipline: The Path to Spiritual Growth* (New York: Harper & Row, 1978), 24–25.
6. Jack Kornfield, *A Path with Heart: A Guide through the Perils and Promises of Spiritual Life* (New York: Bantam Books, 1993), 58.
7. Ben Campbell Johnson, *To Will God's Will: Beginning to Journey* (Philadelphia: Westminster Press, 1987), 52.
8. This exercise is based on an exercise by Ben Campbell Johnson, ibid., 54–56.
9. Thomas Moore, *Soul Mates: Honoring the Mysteries of Love and Relationship* (New York: HarperCollins, 1994), 93.
10. Ibid., 95.
11. Edward Schillebeeckx, *Christ: The Experience of Jesus as Lord*, translated by John Bowden (New York: The Seabury Press, 1980), 48.
12. Stephen R. Covey, *The Seven Habits of Highly Effective People* (New York: Simon & Schuster, 1989), 129.

CHAPTER 9

Spiritual Mentoring and the Leadings of the Spirit

William James, who wrote *The Varieties of Religious Experience*, said spirituality is the attempt to be in harmony with an unseen order of things. This longing is in the soul of all mortals, planted there by the divine Creator to help us perceive the reason for our creation. Through the life, death, and resurrection of Jesus, we are called to accept the divinity within us and to grow in the likeness of our Lord, which is to partake of eternal life.

The world view established in the Restoration is that the Unseen is in our favor and is reaching out to help us fulfill our destiny. This outreach comes in many ways. Of special concern to us here is "sensing the leadings" of the Holy Spirit with all the implications of benefit, misunderstanding, and problems. It is somewhat like inheriting money. You can use it well or misuse it. Making these materials available is simply a response to an existing divine initiative. In specific prophetic instruction to the church we have been told:

> I am longing to pour out greater blessings than you have ever known if you, my people, will open yourselves through preparation, study, and prayer...and prepare to receive a renewed confirmation of the presence of my Spirit in your experiences of worship.—Doctrine and Covenants 158:11 b, c

Such counsel summons us to consider the ministry of the Holy Spirit with the growing maturity that arises only from experiences with the "leadings" of the Spirit. We cannot depend entirely on reading books or receiving advice from others to learn about the ministry of spiritual mentoring. Each person must learn in a way that is related to his or her gifts and calling. However, we can support each other in prayer and love. We can provide some guidelines for this process drawn from experience and from the teachings of the great spiritual mentors. But finally, there is no substitute for seeking personal spiritual guidance and also involvement with another person as a co-journeyer and spiritual guide, or with a mentoring small group.

There are potential dangers involved in one-to-one and group relationships. However, there may be even greater danger in interpreting your own spiritual leadings and deceiving yourself with your own biases or emotional involvements and becoming your own god. The benefits of following the counsel and encouragement provided here can be important for your spiritual life and ministry. Focus on the positive elements of spiritual guidance and mentoring, and do not fear. The apostle Paul wrote, "For God hath not given us the spirit of fear; but of power and of love, and of a sound mind" (II Timothy 1:7).

Growing in spiritual insights and skills is a divinely offered opportunity. No mortal can be infallible in spiritual things any more than in other areas of life. We learn by experience and, above all, need loving support in our growth process. Spiritual mentoring can provide that loving support.

There are three sections in this chapter:

• **Part 1 is "Called to a Relational Gospel."** The Christian gospel is not merely some form of knowledge or set of doctrines. It is most profoundly a relationship to Jesus Christ by faith. The relationship we enter by cove-

nant ties us to Jesus through the baptisms of water and
the Spirit. Our discipleship as followers of Jesus then
becomes a spiritual journey, not just an intellectual con-
clusion or a system of beliefs about him. In that journey
with Jesus, and with other disciples, we all need spiritual
guidance in the form of loving support as well as assistance to properly interpret "leadings" from the Holy
Spirit. Such help is called spiritual mentoring.

• **Part 2 is "Spiritual Mentoring."** An explanation
of spiritual mentoring—what it is and how and why to
seek it—is offered for those who would like such assistance in their spiritual life. Not everyone is at a place in
their journey where they feel such need or want to participate in such a relationship. For those who do, this
section will provide valuable assistance for co-journeyers
relating to spiritual guidance.

• **Part 3 is "Relating to God."** Books and writings on
spiritual mentoring deal almost exclusively with the
relationship between a spiritual guide and the person
being mentored. Little is written about how divine guidance is experienced. The materials in Part 3 will be
helpful to those who participate in spiritual mentoring
as well as others. The principles and lessons set forth
provide valuable insights from personal experiences with
divine guidance.

Part 1: Called to a Relational Gospel

Peter and the other disciples were with Jesus almost
daily for three years. During that time they had established in their own minds some identity—a structure of
things they believed. As with us, it was a combination of
what their culture had taught them and the things Jesus
was teaching them. It must have been a struggle for some
of them to find their belief system under constant adjust-

129

ment as they traveled with Jesus. Their background in Jewish culture and beliefs focused very much on the Sabbath—keeping the Sabbath and the well-defined rules of what they could and could not do on the Sabbath. When Jesus broke these rules on some occasions out of need and said, "The sabbath was made for humankind, and not humankind for the sabbath" (Mark 2:27 NRSV), their belief system was, in a sense, under attack. They were forced to examine their established teachings and beliefs and to try to adjust to this new perspective on life as disciples of Jesus Christ.

When their whole world was destroyed at the crucifixion and loss of Jesus, Peter said, "I go a fishing" (John 21:3) or "back to my old life and beliefs." Two disciples on the road to Emmaus said, "we trusted that it had been he who should have redeemed Israel" (Luke 24:20). Their beliefs had been shattered.

When the resurrected Christ came among them, they must have been profoundly excited and relieved to again have a basis for their beliefs and commitments. They probably hoped things would continue much as they had before Jesus' death.

As a result of the ministries of the risen Lord, the little group of believers was established once again and began to multiply. Leadership functioned through Peter, James, John, and later, Paul. Again their belief system was turned upside down.

This time it was more than Sabbath rules. Through the religious experiences of Peter and Paul, God was directing a change in their scripturally commanded dietary laws and in the necessity of circumcision, which had been given through the great prophet Moses as necessary for salvation. (See Galatians 3:10 and Leviticus 11:47.)

Peter and Paul declared that it was no longer necessary to keep those carefully prescribed rules.

Jesus was saying to them again but in new ways, Hear me and follow me. I will lead you along: "I am the way, and the truth, and the life. No one comes to the Father except through me" (John 14:6 NRSV).

This in essence was what Jesus had been trying to help them see from the beginning of their relationship with him. But their Jewish culture bound them to a previously given belief system that had become their identity. This was who they were—a Hebrew people of God with the teachings of Moses and the prophets as a belief system arising out of their history. When Jesus taught them that some of these things were no longer necessary in their new and growing relationship to him and his purposes, some disciples stayed with their old belief system and the security they had there. Others responded to the Lord's call by exercising the faith to continue on their spiritual journey and found themselves increasingly anchored not so much in a system of beliefs as in a person—Jesus. Their gospel beliefs became more relational than propositional, and they remembered the words of Jesus before his death, "I have yet many things to say unto you, but ye cannot bear them now" (John 16:12).

In their struggles they began to understand that as disciples of Jesus, if their spiritual journey was to continue it must be on the basis of God's instruction to them, "This is my beloved Son...hear ye him" (Matthew 17:4). This experience and instruction had come from God to Peter, James, and John on the Mount of Transfiguration where the continuing angelic ministry of Moses and Elias was associated with the work of Jesus. They also had the testimony of John the Baptist. At the baptism of Jesus, John had experienced the same instruction as a basis for his emerging beliefs when he heard a voice from heaven say, "This is my beloved Son...Hear ye him" (Matthew 3:46). Only on the ground of this relationship can the Lord's work progress.

The disciples of Jesus in every age face this same challenge. You cannot confine within a system of beliefs, a book, or three books, the Creator of all life whose work is to bring forth on earth a people in divine "image and likeness," which is the kingdom of God. As that kingdom of God emerges on earth, it will reflect itself in all the structures of society and group life, as well as in personal dimensions and fruits of the Spirit.

Our gospel does not come to us by way of philosophy with its foundations in Greece and the efforts of mortals to systematize their understandings of truth and reality. Our Christian gospel comes to us by way of Palestine and spiritual experiences with the divine Creator. Our Restoration gospel is a call for commitment to a person, Jesus, and to a lifelong spiritual journey, both as individuals and as a people of God, which is well described in the words of Jesus,

> Ye are little children, and ye have not as yet understood how great blessings the Father has in his own hands, and prepared for you; and ye cannot bear all things now; nevertheless be of good cheer, for I will lead you along.... Doctrine and Covenants 77:4 a, b

Classical theologies, process theologies, or any effort to "finally understand" and define what God will do or not do are eroded again and again by experiences with the God who said, "my thoughts are not your thoughts, neither are your ways my ways, saith the Lord" (Isaiah 55:8).

Out of knowing Jesus and being his disciples, we begin to understand that our identity and role are one. It is out of fulfilling our disciple role *with* him (not *for* him) that our identity emerges. Jesus is our identity, the pattern from which we are cut and to which we may participate in bringing forth his kingdom on earth. His ministries are the ministries of his disciples.

Jesus' counsel was quite specific regarding the issues of role, authority, and mission. These words to his disciples as recorded in the Book of Mormon are applicable to his followers everywhere and in every age. They are especially applicable to his Restoration disciples whom Jesus is calling to go forward with him to fulfill divine purposes on earth. Jesus said, "Ye know the things that ye must do in my church; for the works which ye have seen me do, that shall ye also do" (III Nephi 12:34).

How can this be? How can Jesus expect us to do the things he would do if he were offering his personal ministries on earth in our time?

There is recent prophetic counsel to help us understand how to fulfill our callings:

> ...as you gain ever more confidence in sensing the leadings of my Spirit, you will begin to see with new eyes, embrace the truths that are waiting for your understanding, and move joyfully toward the fulfillment of the tasks that are yours to accomplish.—Doctrine and Covenants 159:8

This counsel was preceded by the promptings of the Spirit in 1992, which are personal and full of longing for us to hear, "for the work's sake":

> Indeed, I am longing to pour out greater blessings than you have ever known if you, my people, will open yourselves through preparation, study, and prayer. Look especially to the sacraments to enrich the spiritual life of the body. Seek for greater understanding of my purposes in these sacred rites and prepare to receive a renewed confirmation of the presence of my Spirit in your experiences of worship.—Doctrine and Covenants 158:11b, c

Jesus Christ's work cannot go forward on earth without the response of his disciples and their willingness to follow where he is leading. No power on earth can hold back his work except his own people.

This is a clear call to intimacy with Jesus, to be his disciples indeed. Our efforts to respond to that call to intimacy will lead us to lay aside desires for identity in some office or role or possessions or pride of personal accomplishment. Rather simply "walk in the meekness of my Spirit and you shall have peace in me" (Doctrine and Covenants 18:2n).

The intimacy of our relationship with Jesus ultimately will be the measure of our effective participation in bringing forth the kingdom of God on earth. Jesus is both the model and the means to this end. Jesus' whole life was lived in daily obedience to God. His life is a call to maintain a deep inner seeking and willingness to follow the leadings of the Holy Spirit. The Spirit's guidance may sometimes be over against the willfulness of our limited understanding and intended way of doing.

Jesus' relentless desire was to do God's will. As we are willing to humble ourselves and to repent by daily following this example of Jesus, we will gain "evermore confidence in sensing the leadings" of the Holy Spirit. We will by this means be able to manifest what the meaning of the Restoration is and why it is coming forth:

> that man should not...trust in the arm of flesh, but that every man might speak in the name of God the Lord, even the Savior of the world; that faith also might increase in the earth; that mine everlasting covenant might be established.—Doctrine and Covenants 1:4c, d

Are we not in a similar position to the New Testament disciples following the Resurrection? We thought we knew who we were in the Reorganization. We had defined a belief system that was essentially the rationale for being the "right group" of the scattered Restoration groups after Nauvoo. Our package of beliefs, doctrine, church officers, and history became our "old Jerusalem gospel," to which God answered:

> Some of you have sought security in the words and phrases by which the faithful of earlier days have expressed their knowledge of me. My ways are still the ways of my Son.—Doctrine and Covenants 149:4

The scriptures are important and have their place in fulfilling God's purposes with us. But they cannot take the place of the living Savior who gave them and who will add to them as he leads his people on.

Our beliefs and the appropriate way of witnessing for our Lord were clearly indicated in 1830 through the Restoration prophet: "of tenets [doctrines] thou shalt not talk, but thou shalt declare repentance and faith on the Savior..." (Doctrine and Covenants 18:4d).

In 1838 Joseph Smith, Jr., expressed the gospel relationship this way:

> The fundamental principles of our religion is the testimony of the apostles and prophets concerning Jesus Christ, "that he died, was buried, and rose again the third day, and ascended up into heaven," and all other things are only appendages to these, which pertain to our religion.—*Elders' Journal*, 1, no. 3 (July 1838): 44

God's ways are ever the ways of Jesus Christ. The roots and the "basics" of the Restoration are: "This is my beloved Son...hear ye him" (Matthew 17:4).

If you feel uncertain about what to believe in this time of change and dynamic forward movement of the church—now and always believe in Jesus.

• We believe in Jesus Christ and the testimony of the prophets and apostles concerning him, "that he died, was buried, and rose again the third day, and ascended up into heaven..."

- Our scriptures testify of Jesus Christ—that he gives active leadership to the church today through continuing revelation by the Holy Spirit and inspired prophetic direction.

- The sacramental ordinances of the church and the authority of the priesthood are essential elements in the saving power of the gospel.

- Our primary responsibility as members of the church of Jesus Christ is to bear witness of these truths in word and deed by obeying Jesus' commandments.

- As Restoration disciples of Jesus, "All are called according to the gifts of God unto them..." (Doctrine and Covenants 119:8b) to assist in bringing forth Zionic life—the kingdom of God on earth. This we do individually, as families, and in community.

These beliefs of the Restoration are expressed as "liberating truths of my gospel" (Doctrine and Covenants 155:7) in the midst of the whole body of Christian disciples on earth of which we are a part. We are to be at the "forefront" of the revelation of divine will in replicating the ministries of the Lord Jesus. This we are not wise enough nor faithful enough to do without the guidance of the Holy Spirit. Divine mentoring is promised to those of unreserved commitment to Jesus Christ, a deep humility, and a growing intimacy that arises from seeking with all our hearts to understand and do God's will. This Jesus modeled in his daily walk and ministry.

We know what we believe, and in whom we believe, as Restoration disciples of Jesus. We believe first and foremost in the word of God to our forebears, spoken to the New Testament disciples Peter, James, and John on the Mount of Transfiguration, "This is my beloved Son...hear ye him" (Matthew 17:4). This same divine admonition was spoken from the heavens to John the Baptist as John baptized Jesus in the river Jordan.

This same counsel regarding Jesus and our beliefs came to Joseph Smith, Jr., in the Palmyra grove and comes now to us as Restoration disciples, "This is my beloved Son, hear him." We remember his words, "be of good cheer, for I will lead you along" (Doctrine and Covenants 77:4b).

This promise to lead us means Jesus will give us the leadings of the Holy Spirit, which is the extension of his own life and power to be with us in our journey. Through the Holy Spirit, Jesus will guide and mentor us. When the Lord was asked by Moses the name of the God who was sending him back to Egypt, the answer was "I AM"— the one who will be there with you. This same Lord has promised each present-day disciple, "lo, I am with you always..." (Matthew 28:19). To discover what that promise means and how to receive and properly interpret the leadings of the Holy Spirit is the reason for an emphasis on spiritual mentoring. Everyone needs a spiritual friend on whom they can rely to assist them in their spiritual journey and their mission with God's people.

The following explanation of spiritual mentoring and how to participate in mentoring, or guiding, and supporting spiritual relationships is directly linked to our being disciples and the followers of Jesus.

Part 2: Spiritual Mentoring

Response to the call to a relational gospel places us as disciples in the path of unending growth through a personal commitment and relationship to Jesus. This means we will repeatedly find ourselves in the same situation as the New Testament disciples to whom Jesus said before his departure, "I have yet many things to say unto you…" (John 16:12). Emerging consciousness of a larger reality than they had yet experienced was a condition of their discipleship. Not all followers of Jesus were willing to live in this tension of continuing growth. The New Testament records occasions when some who had been disciples turned away from following Jesus because of what they termed "a hard saying" (John 6:60).

The same is true today! The challenge of new revelation from God that does not fit into the constructed reality in which each person views what is acceptable to them demands faith and trust in the God we have chosen to follow. To reject God's counsel, "whether by mine own voice, or by the voice of my servants, it is the same" (Doctrine and Covenants 1:8b) means we either decide to be our own god or to make a god of some other person or belief system we choose to follow instead. There is always an alternative to following Jesus which, according to the scriptures, was a choice even by some of the angels in heaven.

This is one important reason to consider spiritual mentoring. No mortal is infallible in his or her judgment. In the moment of one's struggle with new dimensions of Christian faith and commitment, to have a trusted spiritual mentor with whom to share can be a matter of profound spiritual significance. What is spiritual mentoring and how does one function in that relationship?

The following explanation is taken from the *Congregational Leaders Handbook* (*Christian Mentoring: "Two Models,"* Vision, B–2). There is another form of mentoring, which is excerpted in the appendix for your consideration. In the mentor/ordinand concept, the two persons participating are usually assigned by the pastor.

Disciples as Spiritual Mentors

Mentoring is the specific joining of one person (called a mentor) with another person (called a disciple) in their common journey with Christ in mission. A spiritual mentor shares listening, prayers, knowledge, and support for the enrichment of another disciple's ministry. It is expected that this relationship will also yield positive growth for the mentor as well. In the sharing of each other's gifts, both the mentor and the disciple will find their individual gifts multiplied many times. This exciting journey of mutual support can enrich the ministry of both participants, build up the confidence of the disciple, and significantly expand opportunities to respond to the challenges of discipleship. The primary model for the ministry of mentoring is found in the life and ministry of Jesus Christ.

Jesus mentored the early disciples and shared the unusual counsel, "Verily, verily, I say unto you, He that believeth on me, the works that I do shall he do also; and greater works than these shall he do" (John 14:12). Jesus chose a group of disciples with a variety of backgrounds. He lived with them, walked with them, was available to them, prayed with them, challenged them, and sent them forth to minister. He expressed the central meaning of lifetime companionship. His ministry constantly expanded the disciples' understanding of life regarding others and themselves.

At the beginning of their discipleship, surely none of them dreamed of the spiritual resources that would be available as they faithfully applied themselves to the ministry of witness and service. Their ministry was multiplied by God's grace as it became focused on the model of servanthood seen in the towel and basin at the Last Supper.

The disciples helped people change their lifestyle, belief systems, attitudes toward self and others, and their reason for living. Serving others with Jesus is the lifestyle which mentoring promotes. Spiritual awareness and compassion for others are the center of Christian discipleship.

Mentoring as an integral component of discipleship can enrich the Christian journey. It is doing something *with* another person more than doing something *for* them. The calling and gifts of each person are multiplied by this support system.

The church received prophetic counsel regarding the importance of personal giftedness in 1887 (Doctrine and Covenants 119:8b). This counsel was reaffirmed in 1984 (Doctrine and Covenants 156:9b,10): "I say to you now, as I have said in the past, that all are called according to the gifts which have been given them." In addition, the 1984 revelation also connects calling and giftedness, "This should be extended with prayer and tenderness of feeling, that all might be blessed with the full power of my reconciling Spirit." Calling and giftedness are two vital aspects of every person's discipleship which come into focus in the mentoring process.

What may seem small or insignificant to us is often of immeasurable value to God and to other people. But the ministry of Christ is most clearly shown when a mentor listens, offers the ministry of presence, prays for another, calls and supports another, and is available willingly to another. Spiritual direction means helping as another is guided into the quality of relationship with Christ which the mentor knows from within.

The mentor/disciple ministry modeled by Jesus is vital to the fulfillment of God's calling to the church. It is especially vital in areas where new gifts and new leadership are just emerging. At such times misunderstanding and uncertainty in the journey of spiritual growth are likely. When these situations occur, it is important for the mentor to be a guide and not the decider of direction.

Discovering and helping to release the gifts of others for outreaching ministry is of great significance. Spiritual mentoring and education are the proper response to spiritual uncertainty rather than abruptly shutting off the spiritual exploration of the disciples through criticism and censure. In all of life's journey, each day, each moment is an opportunity to discover and multiply our talents, gifts, abilities, and service. Christian mentor/disciples rejoice in the challenge to unite themselves with Christ and others in a remarkable pilgrimage. This pilgrimage frees people to fulfill their sacred calling in life. This faith-based pilgrimage affirms our oneness with God's most precious gift to all—the Christ. This pilgrimage assures individuals, churches, and communities that they are divinely commissioned to share in multiplying themselves through others. Cultivation of the ministries of the Holy Spirit is essential to this process.

Jesus is the individual expression of what we are called to become in both personal and group life. Spiritual mentoring contributes to the possibility that individuals will become all they are called to be as they look to the example of Jesus. Spiritual mentors are available to assist in the task of discerning divine guidance.

Developing a Spiritual Mentoring Relationship

Spiritual mentoring touches deeply at the core of what it means to be human and what it means to support one another. The relationship is not that of parent to child or teacher to student, but primarily a loving relationship that does what it can to enable another person to grow spiritually. A spiritual mentoring relationship is grounded first and foremost in a sense of friendship, mutual journey, and common discovery. On this journey the mentor as well as the disciple experience meaningful spiritual growth and faith development. Both need to cultivate in each other a daily awareness of Jesus' promise, "I am with you always." The presence of the Holy Spirit fulfills that promise.

The following principles are important to an effective spiritual mentoring relationship:

1. In spiritual mentoring, the mentor needs to be constantly aware that the real comforter in life is the Holy Spirit. The roles of the mentor are helper, enabler, and fellow traveler.

2. Nothing a mentor does is more important than listening. Every disciple needs to speak to others in order to help examine their deepest feelings, fears, hopes, and dreams.

3. Through sensitive listening, a mentor identifies and affirms whatever direction and inspiration is alive and growing in the disciple.

4. An effective spiritual mentor enables the disciple to see rhythms and patterns in life and to discern which past decisions have led to a deeper union with Christ.

5. A spiritual mentor strives to help the disciple interpret experiences in the light of faith, to see life as a faith adventure, and to trust divine guidance in all of life. The call to discipleship is the call to grow, stretch, and risk.

6. An effective spiritual mentor is able to help the disciple avoid difficulties and possible pitfalls in personal spiritual life and development. The mentor also helps the disciple work through difficulties when they occur.

7. A spiritual mentor does not judge but stands with the disciple and loves unconditionally. The mentor always keeps total confidentiality in the relationship.

8. The spiritual mentor sees success in terms of helping the disciple grow in the divine nature and become more and more involved in Jesus' mission.

9. Sometimes the mentoring relationship can be enriched in a small group that meets together on a regular basis for mutual support, uplift, and challenge.

Mentors are open to sharing with others a growing faith in God. They are willing to share their own journey, their own struggles, and to be with each disciple in their own spiritual growth. The mentor may have more experience or knowledge, yet both the mentor and the disciple travel together a road that is uniquely new because they have not traveled it together before.

Individuals may attempt to disqualify themselves from being spiritual mentors by pointing to others and saying they are more profound, more experienced, or more spiritually oriented. This sense of inadequacy, rather than excluding one from the task, is precisely the insight that qualifies one to become an effective spiritual mentor. Effective spiritual mentors experience a growing dependence on God based on the realization that the Holy Spirit is the real comforter and guide in human life.

The following characteristics are provided not as stringent requirements for spiritual mentors, but as qualities to be nurtured in the lives of those who desire to be effective mentors:

• reliance on and sensitivity to the Holy Spirit;

• desire to care for and help others grow in faith;

• consistent application of spiritual disciplines such as prayer, meditation, and study;

- available to others for listening, conversation, shared prayer, or just the quiet ministry of presence;
- mission-minded, open to spiritual guidance; and
- being engaged in servant ministry with others.

How to Get Started

The following suggestions are offered for those interested in identifying and establishing a relationship with a spiritual mentor:

1. Set aside time each day to open your life to Christ's presence through spiritual disciplines such as prayer, meditation, and creative scripture study.

2. Share with other disciples on a regular basis in group worship, study, and service to others.

3. Daily ask God to help you turn your life over to Jesus Christ and become involved with Christ in mission.

4. Observe others who are following Christ in mission. Talk to them about their faith journey. Identify those who are growing in risking faith and response. Ask, "In what ways are you experiencing the living Christ in your life now?"

5. Review the characteristics of an effective spiritual mentoring relationship. Prayerfully select a person you would like to have as your spiritual mentor or with whom you would like to join in a spiritual-mentoring small group.

6. Explain the concept to them and your expectations in relation to spiritual mentoring. Ask them to share with you in your spiritual growth and faith development.

7. Meet with your mentor on a regular basis (weekly or every other week). Develop a relationship in which both of you feel free to discuss your deepest struggles as well as your highest hopes.

8. Expect the Holy Spirit to bless you in some significant ways. Respond in risking faith with a sense of adventure. The Holy Spirit will lead you in your journey together.

Spiritual mentoring is not an "assigned" relationship. Individuals choose their own mentor with the help of the Holy Spirit's guidance through prayer. This relationship may become quite intimate as individuals share their inner struggles on the frontiers of spiritual growth. However, any possible problems may be far greater in trying to "go it alone." Personal biases or emotional attachments may cause us to seriously misinterpret some spiritual leading. In fact, church administrative experience brings awareness of many such unfortunate circumstances in the lives of the membership. Spiritual mentor relationships can be of great value in following spiritually healthy patterns by helping each other learn to "gain ever more confidence in sensing the leadings of my Spirit" (Doctrine and Covenants 159:8) as guidance for everyday life.

As has been written, there is a freedom that is perfect bondage, and there is a bondage that is perfect freedom. As the disciples of Jesus learn the bondage of an ever-increasing confidence in following the leadings of the Holy Spirit, they partake of the divine promise in the relationship of Jesus with God. "[W]alk in the meekness of my Spirit and you shall have peace in me. I am Jesus Christ; I came by the will of the Father, and I do his will" (Doctrine and Covenants 18:2n, o). This is the way the kingdom of God can be brought forth on earth. This is also the way committed disciples can find the appropriate focus of their gifts and callings as coworkers in kingdom building with Christ.

John T. Conway

Part 3: Relating to God

Although many books and articles have been written about spiritual mentoring, few materials deal directly with the leadings of the Spirit and the experiences with God that are the principal reasons for the mentoring. Elbert A. Smith, a man gifted in spiritual relationships, said, "It is one thing to have a spiritual experience. It is a totally different matter to interpret it properly."

There are some understandings about relating to God that can be helpful in the journey of spiritual growth and ministry. The following five points address that relationship and the interpretation of "leadings" of the Spirit.

1. God is self-revealing. We cannot determine the time or nature of revelation. Revelations are related to the accomplishment of divine purposes—the kingdom of God on earth. This Peter described as those who are "partakers of the divine nature" (II Peter 1:4). All things bear witness of God (Genesis 6:66) for those who have eyes to see them.

2. Jesus is both the means and the end for the accomplishment of divine purpose. Jesus modeled for us the "way" by consistently seeking to know and do God's will. As we obey God's commandments we are also told to "live by every word which proceedeth forth out of the mouth of God..." (Doctrine and Covenants 95:3a). This means we are to expect leadings of the Spirit as promised in addition to the scriptural words. Divine help comes to those who are active. You cannot steer a ship unless it is underway.

3. Jesus commanded us to "seek ye first...the kingdom" (Matthew 6:38) and taught us to pray "thy kingdom come..." (Matthew 6:11). As we learn office-centered ministries and the associated skills to perform them, initiative should be taken to perform them. The

146

needy are all around us in the church and community. There is the promise of divine help in this process (Doctrine and Covenants 158:11a, b).

4. How will the promised spiritual leadings come to us? Almost without exception, very subtly! Why would this be true? If God is willing to give divine help for our life and ministry, why not give it very plainly? The reason is that agency or right of choice must be preserved. Neither God nor the angels will violate that relationship.

Can you imagine any more critical time for the recruitment of earthly disciples to advance God's cause on earth than immediately after the resurrection of Jesus? There was great need to regather the scattered disciples and again enlist their commitment to Christ and to the kingdom cause for which he came. What did Jesus do? He walked all afternoon with two disciples on a dusty road between Jerusalem and the town of Emmaus without letting them know who he was. Why? To retain their choice to become involved again with him. Jesus had "all power." He could easily have appeared in some powerful and compelling way to reenlist the commitment he wanted for the emerging Christian movement. But free choice is inseparably bound to growth. Being compelled to do something may lead to conformity, but it does not foster the emergence of divine growth and the fulfilling of our destiny. The choice is always ours.

The Spirit works with us according to our gifts. Truth is light for our path whether studied, reasoned out, or experienced by some spiritual leading—and sometimes found or experienced in the most unexpected moment or way. Jesus has counseled us to "walk in the meekness" of God's Spirit (Doctrine and Covenants 18:2) or in the humble manner in which he sought and received the divine will. If we are not listening *for guidance, we may not be able to listen to* guidance. Sometimes the spiritual leading may come as a thought, other times as a feeling, or through the words from another person. Expectancy will assist us to live "on the edge" enough to be able to hear, most of the time. Many profoundly important spiritual leadings go unnoticed and fall like seeds on rocky soil. However, it is important to remember that God values our mistakes as well as our right choices and alert responses—if we learn from them. With agency we are to "taste the bitter that we may learn to prize the good." Some important lessons come from the painful experience of failure or disobedience. The atonement and love of Christ "covers us" in this place of choice and learning. Alternatives of choice, and sometimes paradox, cause the struggles of growth that are essential to our divine destiny.

5. There are many relational aspects of discipleship. As disciples of Christ we accept the tenet that our God is a great and unchanging being. As we address the concept of God seeking a relationship with us as learning creatures, and as we accept the concept of a spiritual journey, we are actually confessing that we are changeable and are changing.

This confession of our changeableness is probably second in importance only to our confession of belief in God, and in Christ as our Lord and Savior. For the Christian, the confession of the possibility of a need for personal change and growth introduces us to the notion of spiritual journey and shapes our openness to the call of discipleship.

Spiritual mentoring has been articulated as a process of co-journeyers, sharing together in spiritual friendship to help each other (one-to-one or as a group) to hear the Spirit of God in their lives individually and collectively.

It has also been said that the significance of this "hear him" experience in our lives is not just for our personal benefit, but that this hearing brings us into relationship with the Divine, for Christ is constantly seeking to introduce us to the Divine. Therefore, we can come to understand mentoring as introducing others to the divine One, the "I AM." Jesus modeled this role in his own earthly ministry.

The third confession of discipleship is that while Jesus Christ and the scriptures have communicated to us that our relationship with God is, from a human perspective, multifaceted, the fallibility of past spiritual guides has seen God in limited ways. This narrowness has limited our expectations and openness to a richer and fuller discipleship relationship with God.

Being a spiritual mentor is, in some ways, a risky matter, even when one has had years of in-depth intimacy with God and the Holy Spirit. In an attitude of humility, the spiritual mentor realizes that the fullness of God is still unknown to any of us. The hazard is reduced by a great measure if the spiritual mentor understands the multifaceted role of relationships that are involved in our scriptural heritage and in our collective spiritual experience.

God as Lord and Master

For example, the scriptures are clear that God is our Lord, our master (see Isaiah 45:23 and Doctrine and Covenants 41:2a). In our spiritual journey, therefore, we grow to understand and experience a relationship with God in which we are servants to the divine Master. Spiritual mentoring will help us fulfill this important relationship with God through accepting our servanthood and searching together for the arena of our servant calling.

Some mentors may focus totally on this relationship with God. To do that may be suitable for the moment, if one is just becoming a believer. But to stop there is, in some ways, to end the journey and to shut off the opportunity for additional spiritual insight and joy.

God as Parent

Another example of a role relationship found in our scriptures is the relationship of God as a parent to a child (Doctrine and Covenants 77:4). Some spiritual guides confuse this role relationship with the master-servant relationship. To do so is to miss a marvelous spiritual opportunity. The child spoken of in this role relationship is the adult. What makes the role relationship different from the master-servant relationship is the openness to the wisdom and loving nature of a divine parent who is always relating to us to help us become spiritual adults. This is the aspect of God's work in our lives that allows us to utilize our agency. We are invited to freely choose, of our own will and volition, to love God and to do the divine will, to love God's creations, and to, in a beginning way, be creatures made in the divine image.

The role of the spiritual mentor in mentoring this relationship with God is to "midwife" a spiritual growth that brings immense, unspeakable joy to both the human disciple and the Creator. God wants our love because of our freedom to love, not out of fear. In fact, true love, even between humans cannot be forced, ordered, or mandated. Then we get compliance without intimacy. We get stability without peace. We get obedience without growth.

God as Friend and Companion

The Lord Jesus modeled for us a third role relationship (see John 15:15). Christ's purpose on earth is probably only partly clear to even the greatest of scholars. But one thing stands out as an obvious revelation of the Incarnation: God seeks spiritual companionship. God is leading us by the example of Christ and by the Holy Spirit (Comforter) to become mutual friends with the divine Spirit. The spiritual mentor, as a disciple on a spiritual journey, may or may not be fully developed in this role relationship. But the mentor must have faith in this possibility and must struggle together with other disciples to become open to the invitation articulated by Jesus, "I call you not servants...but I have called you friends" (John 15:15).

It is understandable that many disciples find friendship with the Divine to be a difficult consideration in their spiritual journey. Perhaps this relationship is itself a gift of the Spirit and not a goal to achieve or a ladder to climb. If that is so, then the spiritual mentor role is not to offer hoops for the disciple to jump through, or yardsticks for disciples to adhere to. Rather, the mentor becomes an example of a spiritual friend, and as part of the mentor's own spiritual devotions, he or she prays for the disciple's readiness to receive the spiritual gift of the knowledge and awareness of God's friendship.

God as Partner and Coworker

The first three role relationships point directly to the fourth. God has called us all to be partners and coworkers in building the kingdom (Doctrine and Covenants 156:9b). There are many ways individuals can be partners with God. Many people are actually doing kingdom-building work but are not aware of it, nor are they intending that their life activity be done for that purpose.

The role of the spiritual mentor is to be present to individuals—disciples, believers, even nonbelievers—in an attitude based on this call to partnership with God. At this point the spiritual mentor operates out of two important awarenesses.

First is the awareness that God has chosen to achieve divine ends through created beings. God is able and, in a human sense, needs or lacks for nothing. God is no less God if we do not obey, believe, love, choose, or do the divine will. It is, therefore, an awesome mystery that God calls all human creatures to build the kingdom. However, in light of the discussion of the first three role relationships, the spiritual mentor must be convinced that "all are called," that "all have gifts," and the purpose of this truth is that God invites each and every person ever created or that ever will be created to share in the cause, share in the work, share in the way of eternal life.

There is much that is beyond our grasp in this call to partnership. But the simplicity of the truth that must guide the spiritual mentor is that God stands ready, always, to hear the petition and requests for assistance from partners who know the divine One and know what God is attempting to accomplish. Perhaps God is most joyful when a servant, who is a freely choosing adult "child," also feels deeply a mutual companionship and turns his or her eyes to God saying, "God, you and I can do this thing that I see needs to be done; let's do it together."

For that matter spiritual mentorship is itself a partnership with God. Learning how to relate to God, our Creator, to ourselves as growing children of God, and to others around us is a challenging and exciting spiritual journey.

Experience with God

Those who have consciously identified the movement of God's Spirit in their lives know their lives are profoundly marked by those moments of divine revelation. Their experiences with God are treasured and remembered again and again. We can also greatly benefit from the experiences of others as they testify of God's blessings, which may come even as rebuke or correction, as is clearly indicated in some of the Doctrine and Covenants revelations (see Doctrine and Covenants 2).

If you have not been able to identify in your life some experience with God by the Holy Spirit, it does not mean God loves you less. God loves all equally. Our gifts differ. That does not mean that one person's divine giftedness is better than another. It is simply different. The Lord works with each person differently. However, as common members of a divine family, we belong to each other and can benefit from each other's present-day experience with God if we are willing to share either in mentoring or in simple testimony.

Religious experiences tend to be moments of perception or of divine influence to help posture us, somewhat like a physical education teacher may say, to put your back against the wall and feel what it is like to stand up straight. Those occasions of experience, whatever form they may take, are like snapshots in an album of life's best moments, to remember, guide, and inform our future.

The following experiences or lessons from my experience are recounted simply in the spirit of sharing God's blessings of divine love, nurture, and mentoring care.

> As I was driving one day, a subtle leading of the Spirit indicated I should visit a certain family. This leading was repeated, and each time I said to myself, Yes, I will have contact with them. Right now I must complete this church work in which I am engaged. My activity led to other things, and I had soon put off to another day the visit to the indicated family.

The result was a devastating circumstance in the family I was to visit, which might have been averted if I had responded to the leading.

In response to this, I was deeply disturbed and prayed to God either to guide me in ways strong enough for me to hear or to leave me alone. After considerable prayer and concern about the issue, I was visited by the Divine Spirit which said to me, "The price you pay to be my disciple is the willingness to fail and try again."

I said to myself, I guess that's the only way we can grow. I'll try to respond more readily.

Sometimes we remember our successes, and other times our failures, because of the lessons we learned from the experience. However, one important insight arises out of nearly all spiritual leadings that applies to practically all experiences or responses. *Most spiritual guidance shows us with clarity where we are.* Because we tend to want direction or decisions made for us, we may misinterpret spiritual leadings and bend them to confirm or support some direction we want to go. At this point, a spiritual mentor can help us realize that the Lord wants us to make decisions and is always there to help us see with clarity the circumstances of our situation.

Charles E. Mader
John T. Conway

CHAPTER 10

Report on Ministry of Angels

At the 1994 World Conference the Presiding Bishopric, in consultation with the First Presidency, issued a report on their consideration of the ministry of angels. That report, received by the Conference, is reprinted here.

At the request of the 1992 World Conference, the Presiding Bishopric has given serious consideration to the concept of the ministry of angels. After consultation with many involved sources, and in prayerful consideration of the scriptural references (Doctrine and Covenants 83:4c; 104:10), we offer the following reflections to the Conference.

Some of our literature, and the testimony of a number of people, describes experiences people have had with what they understand to be spiritual beings, sometimes identified as angels. Many other members have not directly experienced such a phenomenon but speak of a powerful sense of God's presence at various times in this life. However it is understood or experienced, the ministry most commonly associated with angels, both scripturally and experientially, is that of support and acceptance. Angelic ministry refers to the expressions of love, watchcare, and reconciliation from both the human and divine.

Perhaps more important, however, is that the ministry of angels is associated with the peaceful acceptance of

155

the decisions of God that are reflected in our lives—sometimes joyfully and sometimes with great sadness—but always with the promise of God's care.

It is both biblical and experiential that people perceive the ministry of angels as they are comforted in their grief, aided in their challenges, confirmed in their worthwhile endeavors, and reassured of the love God has for them. The key to the ministry of angels lies in the gift of divine presence. While some experience this presence in the form of angels, others recount a strong awareness of God's love, and, still others, a feeling of powerful relief in the midst of silence. In all cases, the experience of those touched by God is a feeling of support, encouragement, and acceptance.

The key to such ministry of presence already lies within the purview of the Aaronic priesthood by virtue of their calling to family ministry, conflict resolution, teaching of stewardship principles, and as representatives of the body of Christ to those in need of the assurance of God's love. Seen in the call to the offices of deacon, teacher, and priest, the availability and promise of such powerful presence is described in the scriptures as the ministry of affirmation—the angelic ministries.

Within the scriptures of the church, the specific reference to the key to such ministries remains unclear. Historically, it has been understood as the ability to open the hearts of all to God's presence. Like so many aspects of divine instruction, we are not fully aware of all that lies within such instruction. But the experience of the church has been that over the years we grow into such understanding as we mature, both as individuals and as a church.

People of faith who share their encounters with God's Spirit are expressing deeply personal and individual encounters that are often described to the larger body in a variety of ways. While affirming the burning bush experience of Moses, we also recognize that God addressed others with pillars of fire, blinding lights, compelling voices, and arresting visions, as well as in the less describable experiences of reassuring presence.

It behooves the Aaronic priesthood to concentrate their efforts on embodying the callings of their offices, aware that the experience of angelic ministry lies in the watchcare provided to God's people by God's ministers. We believe firmly in the idea that God is present, and that we experience God's nature in such a variety of ways that all have expressions of this gift.

Great care and effort are being expended to prepare new resources and expand on existing materials in order to support the Aaronic priesthood in their unique and highly significant ministries of presence and preparation.

The Presiding Bishopric

SECTION IV

Outreach and Commitment

CHAPTER 11

Mission, Vision, and Celebration

Central to the significant growth of any organization lies its understanding of its own mission and vision. The following statements have been developed by the Joint Council (First Presidency, the Quorum of Twelve Apostles, and the Presiding Bishopric). These statements relate to the manner in which the church envisions its mission as it relates to today's world.

World Church Mission Statement[1]

We are the body of Christ. His Spirit leads us to proclaim the gospel.

The purpose of the Reorganized Church of Jesus Christ of Latter Day Saints is to help families and congregations develop the likeness of Christ in each person. Such congregations seek to continue Christ's ministries. We embrace an unconditional love for all and seek with them a faithful relationship with God. Our congregations thus become witnesses to God's redeeming presence in the world.

Led by continuing prophetic direction, we affirm truth, embrace all persons as being of inherent worth, and teach a life of stewardship.

We invite everyone to join us in seeking a life reconciled to God, who brings assurance to today and hope for tomorrow.

> ## Mission Statement
> (Short Form)
> We proclaim Jesus Christ and promote communities of joy, hope, love, and peace.
>
> ## World Church Vision Statement[2]
> We believe the future belongs to God and that the promise of God's kingdom shall be fulfilled. We have a vision of that kingdom, where the name of Jesus Christ is truly honored, where God's will is done on earth, where the hungry are fed, poverty is alleviated, sinners are repentant, and sin is forgiven. We believe that love is the proper foundation of our relationship with others, that opportunity to grow in the likeness of Christ should be fostered, and that the resources of the world can be managed to respect and preserve their creation and purpose. We have a vision of a time when all evil is overcome and peace prevails.
>
> Impelled by this vision, we will be an international community of prophetic vision, faithful to the risen Christ, empowered by hope, spending ourselves courageously in the pursuit of peace and justice.

Living Out the Challenge

A teenager stands before a mirror and asks, "Who am I?" No longer a child, not quite an adult. At any moment in time we all know we are "no longer" and "not yet." But who we are in the present moment and who we will be in the future may elude us, and we find the feeling disturbing. The church has been asking this question, as it must from time to time. We can be grateful that our vision and understanding of God expands and changes. Yet, in the process, we feel uncomfortable moving from the familiar to the "not yets" of the future. We ask the gnawing questions, "Who are we?" and "What are we becoming?" When we project ourselves into the future with dreams, we create a hope that can become reality. Such hopes are based in our most inspired moments. Believing that God guides our future, we realize we also participate by living out the dream and the possibilities. Statements of vision and mission help us answer these questions that define our purpose, direct our efforts, and guide our dreams.

Vision is the distant point on the horizon that guides us through the desert. It gives us a point to check periodically to see if we are moving in the right direction. It is a statement of the dream we have as a people. It shows us the direction we want to be growing. It lifts our vision above our individual footsteps to know that what we do as individuals and congregations and World Church is purposeful. It gives direction that reflects our best understanding of the kingdom of God on earth. It brings purpose and meaning that, when lived out, creates a deep sense of joy that can be found only in response to the love of God. In all we do we look to the example of Jesus who proclaimed his vision when he picked up the book in the temple and read, "The Spirit of the Lord is upon me, because he hath anointed me to..." (Luke 4:18).

We would do well to commit our vision, mission, and celebration statements "to memory." It is probably more important to commit such statements "to life." They are not merely for reciting, but for living out. But it is in daily living that such statements of our best ideals begin to be challenged. When our love is not sufficient to include the person who has just stepped on our toes or our best ideas, we need to stop a moment to check that point on the horizon and continue with an understanding of who and whose we are.

We are not individuals struggling with life alone. We are connected to others by the web of life—interdependent on each other for life itself, dependent on community for our humanness.

Lyle Schaller, a chronicler of modern church society, suggests that one of the major identifying factors of young people is the group or "tribe" where they belong. This may be a club, a gang, a team, a musical group. What we can see most clearly in youth is true of everyone. Humans seek identity in community. Each of us yearns to be someplace where we feel we belong, a place where everybody knows our name, where we are missed when not present, where there is a place for us to be ourselves. The church can be such a place.

If the church is to be a place to belong, it must also have open doors or it becomes no more than a clique or social club. ***The body of Christ is inclusive, welcoming all into the presence of Jesus Christ.***

It is easy to be comfortable in a group of people very much like ourselves—people with shared values, experience, and culture. This kind of community demands little of us. But we are called to be an *inclusive* community, recognizing that Christ's love extends to all people in all parts of the world. Jesus Christ modeled such inclusiveness. He ate dinner with the despised tax-collectors. He empowered the common people. He defied tradition in ways that allowed women to become disciples and evangels.

There are times when our intent is to be inclusive, but we have unconsciously set up barriers that make it difficult for people to enter the community. We (the insiders) may not know their (the outsiders) culture. In every community there are unspoken rules and expectations—when to sit, when to stand, when to speak, to whom to speak, how to speak, how to dress, and on and on. Newcomers also have their own set of rules and expectations. Often the task becomes too great and the community either closes its doors or the outsider feels too uncomfortable to continue to try to belong.

The members of the Aaronic priesthood carry a special responsibility for removing barriers to entry into the community of Christ. Gifted with hospitality and friendship, Aaronic priesthood help to create an atmosphere of openness to others, while helping to interpret the expectations of the community. They will see that special needs are met. This might mean anything from a large-type Sunday bulletin or handicapped accessibility to appreciation of cultural differences in worship.

But we are not just any community. It is significant that we are called to be the body of Christ. This is our identity. With this identity comes the privilege and responsibility "to help families and congregations develop the likeness of Christ in each person." This happens in many ways. It happens because people are called through worship that is relevant to life and witnesses of the love of God. It happens because people experience spiritual nurture. It happens because it is a place of learning, repentance, and growth. It happens where people are invited to be part of the decision-making process because each person is important. And it happens because people are challenged to use their best gifts and unite with others in meaningful mission.

In his talk at the 1994 World Conference, Leonard Young made this affirmation: "The day of the program-focused church is in twilight; the day of the relational church is beginning to dawn."

Personal ministry is not a side issue in the work of the church. It is at the very heart. What we do as interpersonal ministry we do as disciples who are about the work of the Lord. It is something we all do as the body of Christ in response to God's love. Some of us are only beginners while others have more maturity but continue to learn. It is the joyous response of disciples.

The mission statement talks about "unconditional love for all" and the vision statement says, "We believe that love is the proper foundation of our relationship with others...." This is where we start. Love is our teacher, our motivator, our tool, our reason, our hope. We learn that kind of love by connecting with its source.

What interpersonal ministry seeks to do is to "develop the likeness of Christ in each person." To grow in the likeness of Christ is the essence of healing and wholeness. We are called to be like Christ. When we are in healing relationships with others, we are living in the likeness of Christ. In this we find our purpose and calling. The church recognizes that we do not do this alone. We offer our ministry as members of families and congregations. We are guided and supported by individuals and by communities. We are guided and supported by God's presence through the Holy Spirit.

Phrases such as "unconditional love for all" or "all persons as being of inherent worth" indicate an attitude we have toward all other people and ourselves. We are an "international community of prophetic vision." As such, the vision we hold and the mission we live out will reflect an international perspective. Where we as individuals lack this perspective, we are challenged to look beyond our own shores and borders to appreciate life as it is experienced by others in homes and cabins and huts far from our own.

We are helped to remember that God's love encompasses each person. The way we see others may be quite different from the way the Divine Creator sees each one of us. Our challenge is to see others with Godlike love.

We also remind ourselves that God is ultimately responsible. None of us is totally responsible for anyone's life, but we can be a source of strength and hope for others as they experience our presence as a safe and supportive place.

To live out this vision may very well be beyond our abilities as humans with our self-centered agendas. Such a vision calls out the godliness in us—that part of us that is spiritual and divinely inspired. But when we are Christ-*centered*, unbelievable things are possible. After all, it was the man Jesus whose call to discipleship changed the course of history and who speaks to people across the centuries.

We are a people who live in mission. What do we do? *"We proclaim Jesus Christ and promote communities of joy, hope, love, and peace."*

To join with others to use our gifts in the ministry of Christ brings a quality of joy that can be experienced in no other way. This we celebrate in the community of Christ. Our statement of celebration is this:

> We are endowed with the freedom and the ability to know and to serve God. Affirming our joyful kinship, we seek to accommodate the diversity of our lives, finding in our special and individual gifts and talents the meaning and great joy of accepting love.[3]

Darlene A. Caswell

Notes

1. *Congregational Leaders Handbook* (Independence, Missouri: Herald House, 1994), *Communities of JOY*, A–7.
2. Ibid.
3. Ibid.

CHAPTER 12

Stewardship Ministries

Living a Firstfruits Lifestyle

Today, one of the exciting elements of the Communities of JOY emphasis throughout the church is the acknowledgment of a "firstfruits lifestyle." We as individuals, like our congregations, have been uniquely called to a specific mission at this time and place to discover and then live out our life's stewardship. It is a challenging process. God has asked us to give our first and best gifts of time, talents, and treasure according to the potential placed within us. And where does God expect us to live out our personal and corporate stewardships? In those places that we occupy daily—at school, the office or factory, the store, over the back fence, at a friend's, at the hospital, as well as at church. That's where we are called to be stewards.

Personal/Family

Becoming a Christian Steward
- Make the decision to be a Christian steward.
- Associate with others who will support you in your decision.
- Be patient, yet persistent.
- Begin to see the role of Christ in all you do—all the decisions—large and small.
- Listen to the testimonies of others.

- Establish/define values to guide your planning and decisions.
- Prioritize, and establish a sense of joy.

> J—(Jesus)
> 0—(Others) = BALANCE!
> Y—(YOU)

A definition of Christian stewardship affirmed by many people in the Reorganized Church of Jesus Christ of Latter Day Saints is this: Christian stewardship is the practice of systematic and proportionate giving of time, abilities, and material possessions based on the conviction that these are a trust from God, to be used in divine service for the benefit of all humankind in grateful acknowledgment of Christ's redeeming love.

Stewardship as a personal response. True Christian stewardship, then, is a personal response to God, growing out of one's gratitude for God's gift of physical life through creation and spiritual life through the gifts of grace in Jesus Christ.

One of the key concepts in understanding the Christian gift-giving/receiving relationship is the love of God:

> For God so loved the world, that he gave his Only Begotten Son, that whosoever believeth on him should not perish; but have everlasting life. For God sent not his Son into the world to condemn the world; but that the world through him might be saved.—John 3:16–17

Another key concept is the response of the steward:

> Stewardship is the response of my people to the ministry of my Son and is required alike of all those who seek to build the kingdom. The spiritual authorities are urged to so teach with renewed vigor in recognition of the great need, and let nothing separate them from those who have more specific responsibilities in the temporal affairs of the church.—Doctrine and Covenants 147:5a

Christian living at its best is simply a response to God's gift. All of our lives belong to God, making us stewards. Our task in life is to manage what belongs to God. All our possessions, time, equipment, talents, and gifts are on temporary loan from God.

The Old Testament Background. The Old Testament proclaims a major truth in Psalm 24:1: "The earth is the Lord's, and the fulness thereof; the world, and they that dwell therein." The familiar text succinctly gives foundation for our becoming stewards.

The Parables of Jesus. Perhaps the richest source of teaching about stewardship in the scriptures is found in the parables of Jesus. He related the precepts to the ultimate meaning of life, which closely parallels the major Old Testament conclusions.

In the parable of the talents (Matthew 25:14–30), Jesus spoke of a man going on a journey. Before his departure, the man called three trusted stewards and gave them instructions about managing his property while he was away. Two of the three made plans. They did long-range planning before they invested. They were successful and were amply rewarded. The one who planned the most was the one most amply and generously rewarded. One failed completely because he failed to plan. Some of the harshest words in the New Testament are directed to the one-talent steward whose lack of planning brought forth the owner's ire. The inevitability of judgment is associated with Jesus' dramatic words, "After a long time the lord of those servants cometh, and reckoneth with them" (Matthew 25:19). Few parables stress planning more than this one. If stewardship means managing all of one's life, influence, and resources in light of an ultimate accounting, it is essential to stress planning. Jesus' emphasis on stewardship involved responsibility and responsible actions.

The point of Jesus' stewardship presentation is that the steward (disciple) is responsible to the owner (God the Creator). This responsibility involves accountability. The parable of the talents and the parable of the dishonest steward (Luke 16:1–13) both support this principle. Jesus also referred to stewardship and the steward in his parable of the dishonest steward and the wise and foolish servants (Luke 12:40–57 IV/12:37–48 others).

The theme of responsible action emerged in many of Jesus' most forceful and familiar stories. We see it particularly in Luke's sequence of parables: the rich man and Lazarus (Luke 16:19–31 IV/ 16:19–31 others), the rich fool (Luke 12:18–23 IV/12:16–21 others), the unprofitable servant (Luke 17:7–10), and the parable of the pounds (Luke 19:11–25). All of these parables stress the final accountability that we have as humans in general, and Christians in particular. That accountability is for our response to the coming kingdom in relation to the use of time, opportunity, and material possessions. We are stewards, either good ones or bad ones.

Creating Vision and Mission Statements
- Approach your firstfruits lifestyle with prayer.
- Receive and review regularly your evangelist's blessing.
- Listen to others you trust and respect.
- Brainstorm with others who will support you.
- Don't ever limit what God and you can do together.
- Don't be limited by what has been done by you and others in the past.
- Examine your interests, talents, skills, gifts, and strengths (and weaknesses).

- Consider the value of workshops and other resources to help you work through the objective process of self-analysis.
- Encourage your congregational leaders to plan a workshop using the resource *Discover and Share Your Gifts* available from Herald House.

Jesus calls us in our day to become more effective in all aspects of living. Developing our own vision and mission statements will help us focus and see the end from the beginning.

What is a vision statement? It is what you want when you think of your highest hopes and best life plans. It is what you understand at this time of your life, to be the possibilities you can achieve as your stewardship in Christ.

What is a mission statement? The mission statement tells what you are, what you desire to do, as in a strategic plan for a Christian life of stewardship.

Your vision and mission statements will help in the process of personal growth. They should help prioritize what you value in life, such as spouse, family, money, possessions, work, pleasure activities, friends and relationships, and church. Searching for unchanging principles brings stability and a greater sense of self-worth. Therefore, think of your vision and mission statement as a tool, similar to a compass that points the way for you.

Principles will apply at all times in all places. These life principles should be found in your vision and mission statements. Principles are self-evident, self-validating natural laws. They provide "true north" direction to our lives when navigating the "streams" of our environment. When we center our lives on correct principles, we become more balanced, unified, organized, anchored, and rooted. We have a foundation for all activities, relationships, and decisions. We also have a sense of stewardship about everything in our lives, including time, talents, gifts, money, possessions, relationships, our families, and our bodies. We recognize the need to use them for good purposes and, as Christian stewards, to be accountable for their use.

Centering on principles found in our vision and mission statement provides sufficient security to not be threatened by change, comparisons, or criticisms; guidance to discover our mission, define our roles, and write our scripts and goals; wisdom to learn from our mistakes and seek continuous improvement; and power to communicate and cooperate, even under conditions of stress and fatigue. So, what are the principles in your life…

- that offer security,
- that offer guidance,
- that offer wisdom,
- that give power?

These four factors are interdependent. When these principles are harmonized, they create the effectiveness of a noble person, a balanced character: a beautifully integrated steward.

Planning a Life of Stewardship over Resources

- Use the Firstfruits Consecration Form. (See *Planning Your Stewardship 2000 Annual Consecration Process*, Vision, F–2 section of the *Congregational Leaders Handbook.)*
- Prioritize your needs and wants (you can't ever have everything).
- Identify your "pearl of great price" (Matthew 13:47 IV/13:46 others).
- Share your plan with others who will support and encourage you.

- Carry your plan with you (keep it visible).
- Be realistic in your planning.
- Remember, you must take one step at a time.
- This is Stewardship 2000, not Stewardship 1995. It may take time to achieve your total plan.
- There are several types of goals: lifetime, intermediate (two to five years), annual, quarterly, monthly, weekly.
- Work at keeping focused.
- Always be willing to give up a second-best goal for the best goal.

All life follows a universal cycle of birth, growth, maturity, and, finally, death. Even the stars follow this unchanging but eternal reality. Humanity's life cycle follows these stages in often complicated and wondrous ways. We are held in awe of each new birth. We share the nurturing responsibilities of growth, and through maturity we recognize the need for dignity and control over one's final stages of life. These stages are the basis for our decision making and planning in life stewardship. It is from this basis that we begin our discussion of financial planning.

A financial plan is a record of our income and expense, but done in advance rather than after the fact. This is usually done by starting with a yearly financial plan, then proportioning to monthly amounts. Writing down the assets you have control over (consumer items as well as investments) and subtracting your liabilities (debts and all other obligations) will start you out with a knowledge base of where you are. Second, you can then plan the allocation of resources (goal setting) to each line-item expense and savings category to establish control.

The record-and-control-type record books available from Herald House will help you keep on course and not overspend on a particular budget item. This leads us to the third aspect of financial planning. Keeping records of income and expenses adds to your knowledge of exactly where your money goes. From there you can decide if that is where you want it to go and make the changes you can to control your finances, directing them to meet your goals.

The basic rules of record keeping are: (1) keep it simple, (2) write it down, and (3) be realistic. The less complicated the process, the more apt we are to do it. Writing it all down gives you something visible to look at to remind you of your goals and stewardship responsibility to God.

The church stands with each member and friend, looking to the challenges and opportunities of kingdom-building, lifting up peace, and winning souls to Christ. This is our call and discipleship—to live a life of stewardship.

Living a firstfruits lifestyle involves commitment and implementation.

- Be assured that God is indeed preparing the way (I Nephi 1:65).
- Have trust and faith; risk responsibly.
- Keep focused on your plans and goals. Saying no really means saying yes to something more important.
- Use rewards as reinforcements.
- Keep asking, "Will this help fulfill my mission?"
- Focus on your blessings.
- Don't be frustrated by temporary setbacks (if you get a lemon, make lemonade).
- Pick up people along the way.

When we give the "firstfruits" of our labors, whether it be in money, the products of labor, or the expressions of our personality in ministry, we need to see the gift as a symbolic act. It enables us to demonstrate that we have committed all aspects of our life to the Lord Jesus Christ and to the cause of the kingdom (Zion). By giving the first and best fruit of our labor, we acknowledge that God is always first in our life.

To be a committed 21st Century Steward, one needs to complete the Firstfruits Consecration Form. It is a personal and congregational planning tool for identifying resources to support the church both here and abroad. Stewards need to view this form as one of the important elements of a dynamic and exciting process of stewardship ministries.

The tithing statement name has been changed to Annual Consecration Summary. All elements are the same for determining one-tenth of your increase as tithing, which you give to support the worldwide ministry of the church. Your tithing and other freewill offerings are included in your plan which is recorded on your Firstfruits Consecration Form.

Evaluate, Review, Reflect (Annual Consecration Summary)

- No plan or practice is ever perfect (especially the first time or two).
- Evaluation produces the seed for *re*-vision, *re*-mission, and adjustments to your plan.
- Focus both on successes ("Give us encouragement") and failures ("Help us discover what didn't work").
- Complete your Annual Consecration Summary.

Stewardship 2000 invites stewards to make an annual plan for their stewardship response of time, talents, and treasure. A review of that plan is encouraged throughout the year. Consecrated stewards could be defined as those committed to a personal calling in their witness of Christ and in daily support of the local congregation's mission. Further, they are called to support through tithes and general offerings their worldwide outreach, sending others where they cannot go.

The guidelines identified on the Firstfruits Consecration Form to qualify as a 21st Century Steward invite individuals to carefully and prayerfully set a personal goal of commitment to a firstfruits lifestyle as a faith response to their stewardship. Specifics will include: commiting up to 10 percent or more of income as soon as possible; completing an Annual Consecration Summary (tithing statement); making an annual contribution to the Temple Endowment Fund; inviting another to become a 21st Century Steward; and completing a Firstfruits Consecration of Time, Talents, and Influence. All are invited to become 21st Century Stewards.

Congregational Goals

Becoming a Christian Steward
(as a congregation)

- Decide to do more than "maintain the store."
- Sense a relationship with other churches, organizations, institutions, and people in the community.
- With the support and presence of the Holy Spirit more can happen than you might think.

Creating a Vision and Mission Statement
(as a congregation)

- Identify the strengths of your congregation (members and friends).
- Define the community needs that are not being met.
- Discover what will excite and motivate your members and friends.
- Make sure *all* can be involved in some way. Use the World Church Vision, Mission, and Celebration State-

ments as a basis. (Note: The World Church Vision,
Mission, and Celebration Statements are available in
Chapter 11.)
- Put your congregational mission and vision statements
in writing.
- Get broad-based participation in developing your statements (don't rush the process).
- Extend your vision statement several years into the
future.
- Discover your niche (don't try to be all things to all
people or duplicate a ministry already being provided).

Planning (as a congregation)

- Have a long-range, interim, and one-year plan so the
program continues when leadership changes.
- Itemize the individual responses from the Firstfruits
Consecration Form to understand the resources (financial and human) available to plan the congregational
program.
- Prioritize your congregation's needs and wants (you
can't have everything).
- Focus on balance: preparing members and friends for
discipleship; serving through outreach ministries.
- Be true to your vision and mission statements.
- Identify some way for everyone to make a significant
contribution.
- Your congregation's plan should be attainable, measurable, worthwhile, and specific.
- Make sure the plan has broad-based ownership (include the leadership team and as many others as possible in developing the plan).

Living a Firstfruits Lifestyle Involves Commitment and Implementation

- Don't be frustrated by unplanned experiences (they might have a higher purpose).
- Keep asking if what is being done is effectively moving the congregation along toward its mission and vision.
- Communicate (make sure people know what's going on and how what they are doing fits in the plan).
- The process/means is often as important as the goals; use it to mentor so new leaders and workers are being developed.

Evaluating/Reviewing/Reflecting (as a congregation)

- Dual purpose: Is the congregation reaching its goal? Are individual members and friends able to use the congregational environment to further discover, develop and dedicate their goals?
- Use periodic checkpoints: congregational meetings; feedback inserts (newsletter, bulletin inserts).
- Help members and friends understand their Annual Consecration Summary (encourage discussion with key related leadership team members).
- Prepare an annual report on how the congregation managed its resources:
  - income statement (contributions/expenses: local church + general church = World Church
  - bequests, memorial funds, and other planned giving
  - use and maintenance of the building and grounds
  - increases in our reserves/contingency funds
  - percent of our budget in congregational outreach ministries (About 10 percent is recommended in the firstfruits lifestyle example.)

Stewardship Outreach

Create Congregational Increase for Support of Outreach Ministries.

- Make plans for outreach beyond the basics of time, talents, and treasure for operating requirements (keep expenses for program *maintenance* to a minimum and save some energies for *outreach* ministry).
- Be in the world, but not of it (Doctrine and Covenants 128:8b); be the leaven (Matthew 13:32 IV/13:33 others).
- Be synergistic: "Where two or three are gathered together in my name...behold, there will I be in the midst of them..." (Doctrine and Covenants 6:15b).

Making a Difference in Your Community

- As an individual (What can I do?)
- As a congregation (What can we do?)

Planning Your Stewardship 2000 Annual Consecration Process

The response to the question "What can I do? is found in involvement in the Stewardship 2000 annual consecration process. Stewardship 2000 is a "firstfruits" approach to increasing resources for the church to meet the challenge of the 1990s and beyond. Incorporated in this process is a variety of helps aimed at assisting individuals and congregations. The intent of Stewardship 2000 is that your congregation implement specific tasks that you will determine. This will allow individuals and the congregation to plan their stewardship response for the upcoming year. Various ideas and resources are offered for implementation, communication, education, and worship. The intent of this section is to review these ideas and resources to allow each congregation to be successful in the Stewardship 2000 process.

Please remember that the materials presented are intended to be used to assist your congregation in meeting your goals and objectives. Congregations should feel free to adapt and modify the timetable to meet their needs.

Organization

The annual Stewardship 2000 consecration process begins with the selection of a congregational Stewardship 2000 coordinator by the congregational leadership team. This person should be capable of organizing the implementation. A great deal of the success of the process depends on this person.

The congregational Stewardship 2000 coordinator should make use of a number of other people in the congregation at appropriate times during implementation. This will serve to reduce the burden on the coordinator, as well as involve others in this part of stewardship ministries. The success of implementing Stewardship 2000 will be enhanced by the involvement of as many in the congregation as possible.

Timeline

A suggested annual Stewardship 2000 timetable will be presented each year as one way a congregation may implement this process.

The congregation should first determine when its First-fruits Consecration Sunday will be observed. It is recommended that this be approximately two weeks before the congregation considers its budget. This allows the leadership team to use the expected consecrations of members and friends as a tool for their budget planning.

Again, the congregation should feel free to adapt the timetable to best minister to the congregation's needs.

Early discussion and education should be an important part of other congregational activities to enhance the effectiveness of the Stewardship 2000 process. Communication, education, worship, and visiting are areas for special consideration and are discussed in more detail in the paragraphs that follow.

Communication

Communication is a critical element of the Stewardship 2000 process. Initial communication is through announcements and other promotion. These announcements should continue throughout the process as appropriate and should inform the congregation about the progress in the process. When distribution of the Stewardship 2000 materials begins, the congregation then will be ready to receive it.

The distribution of letter/information packets and bulletin inserts is a major part of the fall implementation. Distribution should be in person during Sunday or midweek services or by a short visit. Hand distribution is encouraged because it is more effective than mailing; however, because the material needs to be received at specific time intervals, mailing may be necessary in some cases to make sure everyone receives it. Please remember that the materials presented are intended to be used to assist your congregation in meeting your goals and objectives. Congregations should feel free to adapt and modify the timetable to meet their needs.

In addition, posters and banners may be used to add emphasis. Some congregations have also found that posting a 21st Century Steward Update on the bulletin board is an effective way of helping to keep the congregation informed of progress toward the congregation's goal.

The goal during this part of the Stewardship 2000 process is for as many members and friends as possible to complete their Annual Planning and Commitment Guide, the Firstfruits Consecration Form. This will benefit individuals as they focus on their planning. By establishing your yearly congregational goal for the number of 21st Century Stewards as high as is realistically possible, the congregation will benefit by being able to approve a congregational budget that you know is attainable based on a large number of commitments.

Follow-up materials have been developed for use in conjunction with the stewardship emphasis Sundays. These will benefit each individual and the congregation as you focus on managing the plans and commitments made during the fall implementation.

Each congregation will find different ways to effectively communicate Stewardship 2000. A most important factor is to use those methods that best meet the needs and provide stewardship ministry to your congregation.

Education

Stewardship education is part of the fall implementation and is also intended to be available as part of the congregation's ongoing activities. All of the Stewardship 2000 materials are to be used to help individuals and the congregation improve their ability to be effective stewards. This includes all areas of our stewardship: time, talents, and treasure. The following is included to help people become better informed about the different facets of stewardship:
- Weekly and follow-up distribution materials
- Overview brochure

- *Stand in Holy Places*
- *Discover and Share Your Gifts*
- *27-Plus Ways to Increase Giving to Your Church*
- *Family Financial Planning*
- Temple Endowment Fund brochure
- *Stewardship 2000 Kids*
- Offering envelopes (children and adults)
- Firstfruits Consecration Form (children and adults)
- Periodic Stewardship 2000 update

These materials may be used in whatever manner the congregation believes would be most effective. Many congregations use this material in church school classes. *Stand in Holy Places* and *Discover and Share Your Gifts* are especially useful in this format.

Family Financial Planning can also be organized for Temple School directed study credit. This resource has also been used effectively as a community outreach tool by congregations who developed classes and made them open to the community. In these experiences, they used local professionals and experts in the different areas relating to financial planning.

27-Plus Ways to Increase Giving to Your Church is intended to be a congregational resource. Some districts and stakes have held classes to better prepare one or two people in each congregation to use this resource.

With the exception of *27-Plus Ways to Increase Giving to Your Church,* all of this material is recommended for use by individuals to assist them in their stewardship. *Family Financial Planning* is especially recommended to help individuals gain control and improve the management of their financial resources. These helps are available from Herald House or the Financial Development Division.

The overall intent of the educational portion of Stewardship 2000 is to allow people to better prepare themselves to be good stewards over all aspects of their lives. The congregation's role is to assist by providing the resources and a format that best meets the needs of the people in your congregation.

Worship

Worship is an important element built into the Stewardship 2000 timetable. Sermons related to stewardship are possible options for worship and are suggested for several Sundays during the fall implementation as well as the stewardship emphasis Sundays in January, April, and June.

Personal testimonies are another important part of worship and allow individuals to express their own experiences relating to stewardship. Other activities of celebration and appreciation should also be planned as a part of worship. This should include the presentation of heart/dove pins to all youth and adults who complete a Firstfruits Consecration form, and peace seal rings to all children who complete their form and fill six quarter cards for the Temple Endowment Fund. In this way the congregation can see expressions of Stewardship 2000 in its ongoing worship activities.

Visiting

Visits are encouraged to members and friends who have not responded by completing a Firstfruits Consecration Form by two weeks before your Firstfruits Consecration Sunday. Care should be taken that this visit not be allowed to become a fund-raising visit. However, the content of the visit should include reference to their response. Visiting at this point in the process is very important. It offers an opportunity to convey to those who have not yet completed their Firstfruits Consecration Form the importance of their commitment.

It is also suggested that reference to Stewardship 2000 be included in the congregation's regular home ministry program. This will assist in increasing the level of interest. Stewardship 2000 offers a way to discuss providing assistance in many ways not addressed in the past. *As an example:* Those making the visit may identify individuals willing to offer their time and talents to specific congregational needs, as well as those needing assistance in budgeting or preparing a will.

Children's Materials

Stewardship 2000 Kids explores ways to teach children about Stewardship 2000 and firstfruits giving of time, talents, service, and treasure. The materials provide a series of sessions that can be tailored to fit the congregation's needs. An introduction and instruction page are included. Stewardship City may be used as a resource on alternate years.

As part of the Stewardship 2000 Kids program, quarter cards are available through the Financial Development Division. Instructions are provided in the materials on how to use the cards, how to receipt the contributions, and how to order the Children's Peace Seal Ring.

Forms

Various forms have been developed for use in the Stewardship 2000 process. These will help you organize and implement your stewardship emphasis each year. These will continue to be updated and revised from time to time.

1. Firstfruits Consecration Form
2. Children's Firstfruits Planning form
3. Suggested Roles for Implementing Stewardship 2000
4. Order form for Heart/Dove Pin and Children's Peace Seal Ring
5. Children's Ring form
6. Annual Consecration Summary
7. Children's Annual Stewardship Accounting

Use of Forms

1. Firstfruits Consecration Form. This is a planning guide for the individual and the congregation. It encourages annual planning and commitment for members and friends. This form includes time, talent, and treasure for the upcoming year. It encourages all to evaluate their present situation and challenges them to take steps to becoming even more effective stewards in the future. This form will be completed annually by each family or individual and returned to the congregation stewardship commissioner.

2. Children's Firstfruits Planning form. This gives children up to age thirteen their own form to complete as they prepare their firstfruits planning to share their time, talents, gifts, and money for the upcoming year.

3. Suggested Roles for Implementing Stewardship 2000. This resource outlines the responsibilities and gives suggestions for planning a successful Stewardship 2000 process. Depending on the size of your congregation, a single person may be given more than one assignment.

4. Heart/Dove Pin and Children's Peace Seal Ring order form. This is to be used for ordering pins and rings. All youth and adults who complete their Firstfruits Consecration Form making a commitment to becoming a 21st Century Steward should be acknowledged by the presentation of a pin. All children who complete the Children's Firstfruits Consecration form and fill six quarter cards for the Temple Endowment Fund should also be acknowledged by the presentation of a peace seal ring. The rings are for children only.

5. *Children's Ring form*. This form is to be completed in duplicate, with one copy sent in with each ring ordered.

6. *Annual Consecration Summary*. The steward's annual accounting will now be completed by using the Annual Consecration Summary. This form allows the steward to review, analyze, evaluate, and be accountable for the commitment of time, talent, and treasure she or he made using the Firstfruits Consecration Form.

7. *Children's Yearly Stewardship Accounting*. This yearly accounting is designed for ease of use by children as they review, analyze, evaluate, and are accountable for the commitment of time, talents, gifts, and money they made using the Firstfruits Planning Form.

What Is Stewardship 2000?

What do we want to accomplish?

Stewardship 2000 invites everyone to be a 21st Century Steward. Stewards plan, manage, and are accountable for all of their gifts—the totality of life.

The vision of Stewardship 2000 is healthy, vibrant individuals and congregations responding to the call of Christ, freeing their gifts, and living out the mission of the church.

Stewardship 2000 is for all congregations of the church: large or small, rural or urban.

Stewardship 2000 resources are for all ages and stages in life. Let's work together (individuals/families/congregations) to be the best stewards possible:

- to be good planners;
- to be good managers; and
- to be accountable for our stewardship.

As we become 21st Century Stewards, we will benefit ourselves, our families, our congregations, and our world mission. This *ongoing annual personal and congregational stewardship ministries process* will help to create the *ability* and the *desire* for stewards to respond in a firstfruits lifestyle.

Stewardship 2000 was introduced at the 1992 World Conference by the First Presidency and Presiding Bishopric in a special service of celebration.

Stewardship 2000 launches began in May 1992 and were concluded in the United States and Canada in all 129 districts/metropoles/ stakes in March 1994.

The Stewardship 2000 process has been introduced to all 1,171 congregations in the United States and Canada.

Ongoing Stewardship 2000 support will be provided to congregations as they continue to more completely develop the process of enabling their members and friends to live a firstfruits lifestyle.

Action Steps to Consider

For a Successful Stewardship 2000 Process

1. Select district and congregational Stewardship 2000 coordinators (may be the DSC or CSC).

2. Establish congregational goals and objectives to help shape your congregational Stewardship 2000 focus. Adopt budgets that will allow these goals to be achieved.

3. Use Stewardship 2000 resource materials in your Christian education schedule: *Family Financial Planning, Stand in Holy Places, Discover and Share Your Gifts, 27–Plus Ways to Increase Giving to Your Church,* and *Stewardship 2000 Kids.*

4. Initiate a class/educational setting for all adults and youth to completely understand the purpose and use of the Firstfruits Consecration Form. Points to emphasize during the class should include using this form
    a. as a personal planning and commitment tool;
    b. to encourage making specific commitments; and
    c. to identify the human giftedness and financial resources of the congregation.

5. Schedule a *Discover and Share Your Gifts* seminar/class using Panel 2 of the Firstfruits Consecration Form (resources available from Herald House).

6. Order the annual congregational materials from Herald House. Some districts/stakes may want to coordinate the ordering and distribution of the materials, especially for the smaller congregations.

7. Provide a process for home visiting with a general ministry emphasis (use mailings and/or personal contacts) and include the "Annual Stewardship 2000 Timetable" in your congregational calendar as appropriate. The leadership team and priesthood should *lead by example*, making their commitment first, and then share their testimony and support for the ministries of Stewardship 2000.

8. Establish specific ministries that will result in meeting or exceeding your congregational budget as well as your World Church tithes and general offerings and accounting stewards goals.

9. Show and discuss the World Conference budget presentation video at least once each year and invite each family to support the church financially.

10. Emphasize the use of offering envelopes by everyone (adults and children) and distribute stewardship

forms widely. Provide special worship services for the Stewardship Emphasis Days.

11. Publish and distribute reports on the congregational stewardship response (time, talent, and treasure) at every opportunity.

12. Schedule special seminars/classes on stewardship topics for young adults, parents, senior adults, and others.

13. Create/develop an effective team by identifying individuals who have interests/abilities in providing stewardship ministry and by increasing resources (time, talent, and treasure) to support the mission of the local congregation and World Church.

Robert L. Logan

CHAPTER 13

Expansion Ministries

Missionary Vision

The missionary vision of the church is a response to the persistent call of Jesus Christ to proclaim his love and message to all people. It emerges from a profound awareness of the worth of all souls, the eternal depth of God's sacrificial love, and the conviction that the gospel of Christ brings blessing, hope, and peace into human life.

Throughout its history, the church has been challenged constantly to pursue missionary ministry as a priority concern. Jesus instructed his disciples that "you will receive power when the Holy Spirit has come upon you; and you will be my witnesses in Jerusalem, in all Judea and Samaria, and to the ends of the earth" (Acts 1:8 NRSV).

The New Testament records that the first disciples clearly understood that their primary responsibility was to share enthusiastic witness of the resurrected Christ wherever they lived, worked, and traveled. It also affirms that as they were faithful to their mission and diligently bore testimony of Christ, the Spirit drew many people from all walks of life into the expanding Christian community.

Missionary witness was also the keynote of the Restoration movement. Doctrine and Covenants Section 1:4d affirms that a primary purpose of the Restoration is "that faith also might increase in the earth." In Doctrine and Covenants 83:10 the instruction is given: "Therefore, go ye into all the world, and whatsoever place ye cannot go into, ye shall send, that the testimony may go from you into all the world, unto every creature."

Recent revelation urges the church to reclaim missionary ministry as a first concern:

> Know, O my people, the time for hesitation is past. The earth, my creation, groans for the liberating truths of my gospel which have been given for the salvation of the world.... Trust in my promises for they have been given for your assurance and will bear you up in times of doubt....—Doctrine and Covenants 155: 7

Awareness of the yearning of creation for the truths of the gospel to be proclaimed and demonstrated compels the church to reach out in compassionate witness to a world in need.

The World in Which We Live

The world in which we live is in transition and the rate of change is accelerating. In the foreseeable future we will experience the greatest increase in human population since the beginning of recorded history. Most people will live in sprawling urban areas where cultural diversity, social complexity, and the prevalence of human physical, emotional, and spiritual needs will be increasingly apparent. Children, the most innocent and vulnerable of the world's population, will be at the greatest risk as access to adequate food, health care, and educational opportunities becomes more and more limited.

In our society the structures of "religious plausibility" are diminishing. The elements of society that previously encouraged religious practice are crumbling and people are faced with a variety of competing demands on their time and resources. This trend, coupled with the explosion of scientific knowledge and technology that appear to some to leave little room for the "mystery of God," directly challenges the viability of churches and their call to a life of faith, devotion, and service.

Families are the primary setting in which human beings develop self-worth, relational skills, and moral values. Buffeted by social, economic, and religious upheaval, families today are experiencing increased strain and fragmentation. The traditional nuclear family, as previously defined, is no longer the unquestioned norm. Single-parent families, blended families, and other arrangements are increasingly typical. Single adults, by choice or circumstance, are one of the fastest growing segments of the population.

It is apparent that generational differences are becoming more acute, too. The way young adults and youth view life, relationships, politics, and religion is, in many ways, distinctly different from their parents' and grandparents' views. This spills over into congregational life in the form of divergent preferences regarding worship, leadership styles, and approaches to church mission and identity. Unfortunately, a significant number of younger people have already separated from organized religion because of their frustration with the lack of understanding regarding their perspectives, desires, and concerns.

Fundamentally, however, human beings are still searchers for meaning, hope, purpose, and genuine loving relationships with others. There resides in each person an inner yearning for experience with the Divine and acceptance among people who care and understand. The stress, confusion, isolation, and rapid change characteristic of our time heightens the need for people to find that which offers sustaining hope, the experience of true community, and a way to cope with the demands of modern life.

Missionary Priorities

We believe the gospel of Jesus Christ meets the deepest needs of human life and that the church provides the fellowship and ministries that enable people to discover life as God intends it to be. If we take this belief seriously, then there can be no question that the primary purpose of the church is to proclaim the gospel of Christ through personal witnessing and missionary ministries designed to enfold people into the community of faith.

In light of this missionary imperative, the Council of Twelve, in association with the Council of the Presidents of Seventy, have established missionary priorities for the church. We believe these priorities have been formed in response to the prompting of the Spirit and are particularly critical in light of current church and societal trends.

I. *Vibrant Congregational Missionary Ministries*

Congregations are the most essential expression of the church. The primary purpose of congregations is to reveal the personality and ministry of Christ to the world. As such, they are called to be joyful "witnessing communities" that constantly provide the invitation and opportunity for people of all ages to encounter Jesus Christ in understandable terms and to grow in relationship with him.

The World Church "Communities of JOY" emphasis urges congregations to develop a vision of mission based on the needs of members, participants, and residents in the larger community. Mission-driven congregations devote a significant amount of their human and financial resources to efforts intended to contact, nurture, and involve new people in the community of faith.

The Congregation Missionary System (CMS) resource, now available as a booklet in the *Congregational Leaders Handbook* (Mission, C–4), has been developed to provide congregations with a basic plan for implementing effective missionary ministries. It emphasizes evangelism as the practice of hospitality, friendliness, and inclusiveness in the faith community that encourages people to respond to the gospel of Christ and to make life-changing commitments. The CMS outlines a number of practical steps that any size congregation can take to increase participation and expand membership.

The World Church is also engaged in recruiting and deploying teams of congregational evangelism consultants. The primary function of these consultants is to help congregations clarify their vision of mission and create a missionary action plan that can be implemented in a reasonable period of time. Congregational evangelism consultants are trained in group process skills, church growth principles, and congregational missionary strategies. They are also very familiar with a broad array of resources that can be used to augment congregational missionary efforts.

II. *Urban/Metropolitan Area Expansion*

More than 50 percent of the world's population now live in urban/metropolitan areas, and this percentage will continue to increase in the future. The number of "world class cities" (more than 5 million population) has grown from seven in 1950 to thirty-four in 1984. By the year 2025 the total will reach ninety-three. As Ray Bakke, of International Urban Associates, puts it, "You have an urban future whether you like it or not!"

Obviously, a critical challenge before the church is how to express the ministries of Christ in the diverse, complex environs of the cities of the world. The challenge is made more difficult by the fact that most of our current understandings and models for congregational life and church mission evolved in rural settings.

To begin to meet the challenges of urban mission, the Temple Missionary Center is developing an Urban Ministries Satellite Center. The purpose of the satellite center, located in Chicago, Illinois, is to empower urban ministries in the church through extensive networking, research, and pilot projects. It is also involved in providing urban ministry leadership training through conferences, seminars, and internships.

The church is seeking ways to increase the number of professional ministers who are assigned to key urban areas to plant congregations and to establish community development ministries. This will require a conscious shift in the expenditure of missionary funds and the assignment of personnel to target areas.

A program is also projected that will identify and train self-supporting people who are willing to relocate to priority urban areas to strengthen the presence of the church and related outreach efforts. Such people will need to be well grounded in urban mission principles, intercultural ministries skills, and community networking models.

III. *Intentional Intercultural Ministries in All Fields*

It has been said that we will know that it is the twenty-first century when we are all members of a minority group. Internationalization of the population is a companion trend to urbanization and is already evident in many portions of the field. Many of the nations and cultures of the world are now within driving and walking distance. This presents an unusual opportunity for missionary outreach that can bless the church with the gifts and perspectives of numerous cultures.

To engage effectively in intercultural ministries, the church will need to develop greater sensitivity at all levels to cultural issues and concerns. It will also need to develop a team of skilled full-time and bi-vocational missionaries who can be sent to areas of opportunity to coordinate outreach ministries and to plant indigenous congregations. Particular target populations include Hispanics, African Americans, Asians, and various immigrant refugee groups. Church members with a vision for intercultural ministries are urged to develop cultural bridging and language skills.

The Temple Missionary Center is accumulating demographic data and information on ethnic ministries models and strategies. Satellite centers will be created in the field to support intercultural ministry efforts.

IV. *Outreach with Young Adults, Youth, and Children*

Denominational allegiance and natural increase can no longer be assumed as sustaining factors for church membership and participation. Now, more than ever, each generation must be evangelized with relevant ministry. Generational differences require a variety of innovative missionary approaches. Congregations are challenged to risk experimental ministries to identify new outreach models that can be applied throughout the church to reach the younger generations of potential disciples. Again, a primary key to creating such ministries is the development of ministers and leaders who are sensitive to generational issues and are capable of creating pioneering efforts.

It is apparent that one of the interests of young adults and youth is meaningful involvement in the mission of the church rather than just being "spectators" in church services. The evident response needed is the creation of opportunities for young adults and youth to be involved in exciting, demanding missionary and community development projects throughout the world.

Congregations should be places where children are cherished, secure, and constantly mentored in the Christian faith by responsible people. Children's ministry should provide opportunities for children's needs to be met and for children to use their gifts to meet the needs of others. Innovative outreach ministries such as the Young Peacemakers Club and Neighborhood Bible Clubs are showing great promise as the church earnestly seeks ways to ensure the rightful place of children in the center of the faith community.

Of course, in addition to age-specific congregational programs, ministries designed to strengthen families will be a blessing to children and youth. Many families are earnestly seeking for the insights and skills that will help them enrich family life. The creation of effective family support ministries will be a tremendous boost to the outreach of the church.

V. *Church Planting and Expansion in Areas of Opportunity*

Our mission is to take the gospel to every village, city, and nation to which the Holy Spirit calls us and provides opportunity. In response to the Spirit, we sense the call to open the work of the church in new nations and in areas of opportunity in places where the church is already present.

The primary purpose of church planting is to reach people that existing congregations are not likely to reach because of location or dominant cultural or social identity. Because church planting, when properly conceived, is a missionary ministry designed to reach new people, it should not be perceived as a threat or competition to existing congregations. The importance of church planting is underscored by the fact that expanding churches (denominations) are those that are constantly opening new congregations.

There are numerous church planting models and approaches, depending on the target audience for a new congregation. The church may need to establish some very large, multi-service, "mega" churches in order to reach some people, especially segments of the young adult population. Some people who have been "turned off" by existing churches will be reached through networks of outreach groups that specialize in relational small group ministry.

Any church planting strategy requires missionaries who are trained in church planting skills and matched to real opportunities. The World Church missionary strategy includes developing a team of church planters and providing priority missionary development funding to church planting projects throughout the world. It also includes identifying our current network of members living or traveling frequently to priority areas and training them in missionary and church planting skills.

The Temple Missionary Center is sponsoring a Church Planting Satellite Center in the Southeast Field. This satellite center has been leading the way in church planter training and promoting projects that demonstrate the principles of successful church planting.

The Link to Aaronic Ministries

The World Church missionary vision and priorities have numerous implications for Aaronic priesthood members. The fundamental purpose of priesthood is to bear witness of the love of God and the saving grace and sacrifice of Jesus Christ for each person. It is a call to bear the message of salvation to the world and to win people to Christ. Aaronic ministers, like all priesthood, are first and foremost representatives of Christ. They are to concern themselves continually with the welfare of all people in every place and condition. Aaronic ministers are to invite people to come to Christ through demonstrating, teaching, and preaching the fundamental gospel principles of faith, repentance, baptism, and lifelong commitment.

Because Aaronic priesthood are to minister primarily in established congregations, they are particularly vital to the achievement of the first missionary priority: the creation of "vibrant congregational missionary ministries." To this end, each member of the Aaronic priesthood should be thoroughly grounded in personal witnessing skills and well acquainted with the *Congregation Missionary System* and other missionary resources.

The successful implementation of the Congregation Missionary System and other outreach efforts is dependent on the ability of the congregation to establish a caring environment in which people are welcomed, accepted, and assimilated into the faith community. The CMS describes ways to prepare the church physically, attitudinally, and spiritually to provide relational, Christ-centered, people-first ministries that affirm the worth of individuals and reveal God's love for them in tangible ways.

Preparatory ministries such as the upkeep of the church facility, the placement of directional signs, the availability of a clean, well-equipped nursery, and the care of congregational worship, fellowship, and learning spaces create the vital impression that the congregation is expecting new people to come and share.

One of the most important missionary activities of any congregation is a guest (visitor) welcoming and follow-up ministry. Aaronic ministers should take the lead in assuring that the needs of guests are anticipated and that each one is received hospitably. A primary focus of this welcoming ministry should be to learn the names of people and to discern any immediate needs the congregation might be able to meet. The spirit and activity of Aaronic ministers should always leave the impression that each person matters to God and to the church no matter what his or her background or need is. No one should pass through the doors of the church unwelcomed or untouched by caring ministry.

Aaronic ministers can also be involved in other congregational missionary ministries according to their interest, ability, and willingness to prepare. Possibilities include giving leadership to: prebaptismal classes for children, seekers classes for older youth and adults, witness support groups, home missionary meetings, small group ministries, and new member nurture ministries.

Each Aaronic priesthood office also has a particular contribution that it can bring to missionary outreach. As the church intensifies its outreach to the larger community, we will increasingly come in contact with people from all walks of life. Because of their particular calling, deacons should identify closely with the discouraged and powerless in the community. The "Plan for Service" for the deacon states:

> The deacon identifies closely with the poor, the sick, the helpless and needy, and assists them in every way possible to meet their needs. The deacon is their advocate and presents their needs to financial officers if financial assistance is required, the pastor and elders for spiritual ministries, the priests and teachers and others for home ministry and friendly visits.—*Guidelines for Priesthood: Ordination, Preparation, Continuing Commitment* (Herald House, 1985), 80

In this mode of ministry, deacons can truly be "the hands of Jesus" and provide the initial witness that God is concerned about all people. There are numerous examples of how compassionate response to immediate need became the prelude for sharing the gospel in all of its temporal and spiritual dimensions.

Regular participation in the faith community is a particular concern of Aaronic teachers. The focus of this concern should not be limited to the membership but should be extended to all participants and potential members. If anyone stops participating or becomes sporadic in attendance, the teacher should contact them to provide sensitive support and encouragement. Teachers should especially monitor new members to ensure that they become fully assimilated into the congregation and have a genuine sense of "belonging" to the faith community. Also, particular attention should be given to people experiencing any kind of life transition to ensure that appropriate ministry is offered and that a time of crisis does not precipitate separation from the congregation.

The growing cultural, social, and religious diversity in society will have a definite impact on the church. As congregations begin to reflect the community more, they will have to deal with diversity in the fellowship. Diversity can be an enriching experience or it can lead to stress and alienation arising from misunderstanding, fear, and prejudice. As congregational peacemakers and reconcilers, teachers can play a critical role in helping the church accommodate and celebrate human diversity in Christian community. This responsibility will require teachers to gain additional expertise in conflict mediation, cultural sensitivity, and community-building skills.

As mentioned previously, families are experiencing tremendous stress and change. The priest is called to be particularly concerned about the quality of family life in the congregation and the community. This includes encouraging regular church participation, teaching the principles of healthy family relationships, and being familiar with personal and family counseling services.

Family ministries become significant missionary ministries when they are available to all family units with whom the church has contact regardless of membership status. For example, sponsorship of a parenting seminar open to the community will not only benefit members but may provide contact with new families as opportunities for sharing the gospel. A congregation that provides a strong, comprehensive family ministry program will be attractive to those who are struggling to secure and enhance their family life in today's world. Priests should advocate and coordinate the creation of such ministries.

The sacraments witness the presence of the living Christ in the church. Priests are authorized to administer the sacraments of baptism, the Lord's Supper, marriage, and ordination of other Aaronic ministers. When these sacraments are presented with sensitivity and meaning, recipients and observers experience a call to strengthen their commitment to Christ and the church.

As sacramental ministers, priests should always be alert
to opportunities to bear witness of Christ in these sacred
rites.

Conclusion

The stated mission of the church is to "proclaim Jesus
Christ and to promote communities of joy, hope, love, and
peace." For the church to fulfill this mission it will need
to be very intentional about missionary and community
outreach ministries. Aaronic ministers are key players
on the missionary team and they can be involved in a
number of important expansion ministries. The basic
calling of all Aaronic ministers is to contribute to the
creation of congregational climates that value all people,
that are attentive to physical and spiritual needs, that
introduce people to the basic principles of the gospel, and
that invite them to come to Christ through baptism and
active church membership.

Stephen M. Veazey

CHAPTER 14

Communities of JOY

As the church looks forward to the beginning of the next millennium, we must continue to respond to the call to "go and make disciples." In this process the Aaronic priesthood will play a key role as its members help to develop and support the ministry of local congregations. Each congregation is an essential avenue for ministry to its community. The Communities of JOY emphasis focuses on enriching congregational life and assisting in the process of transforming communities into places where the kingdom of God can be seen and felt in everyday life.

Joy is not the result of a program or a directive. Joy is the fruit of the Spirit which results in a sense of community shared. Because members of the Aaronic priesthood are primarily congregational priesthood, they carry much of the responsibility for building relationships within the church community.

The Communities of JOY emphasis focuses on three primary dimensions of congregational life:

- vision,
- mission, and
- celebration.

The church depends on the rich ministry of its Aaronic priesthood members to set the example of what effective ministry can do for the church and the world and to bring the church together in witnessing of our faith in the Lord.

A Model for Congregational Life

The congregation ministers in three dimensions:

The JOY of...

	VISION Inspiring faithful leadership	MISSION Expressing powerful discipleship	CELEBRATION Affirming joyful kinship
Central Focus:	Jesus Christ centered	Outreach oriented	*YOU* are an important part of the family of God
Joyful Affirmations:	Being servants of Jesus Christ	Reaching out to others	Rejoicing in the body of Christ
Personal Ministries:	Planning, enabling, leading, imagining, and serving	Witnessing and community involvement	Studying, praying, visiting, reconciling, and nurturing
Congregational Ministries:	Communication, leadership, and stewardship	Missionary witness, compassionate service, and community development	Caring ministry, education, and worship

The victory of Jesus Christ calls us into a celebration of freedom and acceptance. In this victory, and in the recognition of our personal call to respond to God's love, the joy of the gospel is revealed.

> **Theme Scripture:** "For ye shall go out with joy, and be led forth with peace."—Isaiah 55:12
>
> **Story Image:** The story of the "Woman at the Well" exemplifies the excitement and transformation that occurs when we receive the Master and share the joy of the good news with others.—John 4:1–42

The church is centered in the life and ministry of Christ. Believing the future belongs to God, we envision a kingdom where God's will is done on earth, a kingdom in which, and through which, the body of Christ enjoys the communion of the community. To that end, we acknowledge our response to Jesus' life and ministry and find it in vision, mission, and celebration.

Vision

Recognizing that Christians are called to envision God's future, we foster the image of eternal hope, boundless joy, and inspired leadership. We envision a kingdom in which God's will is done on earth and foresee the church as a community of joy, in which the call to servanthood is courageously empowered in the pursuit of peace and justice. Impelled by the vision of Christ's life, we portray the future as a world in which the hungry are fed, poverty is eliminated, sinners are repentant, and sin is forgiven.

We accept both the commission and the cost of discipleship as we center our lives on the mission of Jesus Christ. We acknowledge the need for stewardship of God's world and accept responsibility for the preservation of creation. We envision an outpouring of love to the larger community. As Jesus washed the feet of his disciples, we, too, can find fulfillment in the ministry of servanthood.

Theme Scripture: "Where there is no vision, the people perish...." —Proverbs 29:18

Story Image: As we consider the parable of the mustard seed we acknowledge the power of our faith to grow and to strengthen and expand our ministry.—Matthew 13:30–31

Story Image: Lehi and Sariah, accepting God's direction and acting with faith in the future, leave all behind and take their family into the wilderness.—I Nephi 1

Inspired by the stories of Jesus as the Shepherd, we seek to be an international community with prophetic vision. We affirm our conviction in the expectation of new horizons. As the Spirit continues to speak and empower us, we move toward redemption. Accepting God's direction and seeking the divine endowment of our spiritual authority, we plan for and serve in the community with faithfulness.

Mission

We are a people of mission who find in the body of Christ the living, breathing embodiment of the will of

God. Our mission lies in expressing powerful discipleship and in communicating the expectation of spiritual maturity and divine promise to all people. Aware of the pain and woundedness of all people, we respond by expressing unconditional love for everyone and seek for them a faithful relationship with God.

The world God has created is our expanded congregation, and it is in the larger world that we will find compassion, justice, and the expression of individual and group worship. Acknowledging the sacramental nature of all creation, we recognize there is no part that is to be despised, no creation that is not good, and no labor that is menial.

Theme Scripture: "All are called according to the gifts of God unto them."—Doctrine and Covenants 119:8b

Story Image: Just as Jesus called ordinary people to be disciples (John 1:35–42), we seek to be open to every individual's uniqueness and every congregation's difference as we respond to God's love.

We find in the Crucifixion the principle of Christ's penetration into the barriers that alienate the human community. Our mission lies in reaching out in witness of God's reconciling love and thus harmonizing individuals with God, nature, and themselves.

Celebration

We are endowed with the freedom and the ability to know and serve God. Affirming our joyful kinship we seek to accommodate the diversity of our lives, finding in our special and individual gifts and talents the meaning and great joy in the warmth of accepting love.

Called to fuller understanding through study and faith, we seek the implementation of God's will in our ministry and in our lives.

Quickened by the Holy Spirit we rejoice in love, joy, peace, mercy, gentleness, meekness, forbearance, temperance, purity of heart, and faithfulness. We respond and celebrate our freedom through study, prayer, visiting, and nurturing. In joy we seek to be God's people and share in divine redemption, so the work of the Lord can be accomplished.

The message of the gospel of Jesus Christ is joy. Being a people of God we are called to articulate this joy to our communities—and to the world.

Theme Scripture: "...he hath anointed me to preach the gospel to the poor, he hath sent me to heal the brokenhearted, to preach deliverance to the captives, and the recovering of sight to the blind; to set at liberty them that are bruised."—Luke 4:18–19

Story Image: As Hannah's appeal to God for a son expresses joy and faith in the future (I Samuel 1:4–28), it also calls us to remember the grace of our Lord and the promise of the Holy Spirit to be with us.

Story Image: As God called Paul (Saul) on the road to Damascus (Acts 9:1–20), we also are called to be God's people in Communities of joy.

WORLD CHURCH THEMES:
1995–2000

Emphasis: Communities of JOY!

Theme
Scriptures: "For ye shall go out with joy, and be led forth with peace."—Isaiah 55:12

"...to bring good news to the poor, to proclaim release to the captives and recovery of sight to the blind, to let the oppressed go free, to proclaim the year of the Lord's favor."—adapted from Luke 4:18–19

Image:

The Communities of JOY emphasis is focused on raising congregational self-esteem, teamwork, competence, and success. A scriptural image that models this emphasis is found in the story of the "Woman at the Well" (John 4: 1–42). This story begins with Jesus using a simple request for drinking water to open a dialogue with the woman [**relationship building**], continues as he helps the woman to confront her real-life situation [**evaluation**], goes on as the Master asks her to see life differently [**transformation**], and concludes with her excited efforts to share the good news with her friends and family [**witness and community development**].

Ministry Concerns and Issues:

The model of congregational ministry in 1995 and beyond centers on ministering with Christ. These emphases should focus on the central concerns, hopes, and dreams of the emerging generation of church members. After careful analysis and feedback from young adults regarding their concerns for ministry, the following issues have been identified as timely focuses of ministerial concern:

1. personal spirituality and an awareness of life as a journey of growth and maturation;

2. compassionate community service and transformation;

3. regard for our stewardship of the earth;

4. new, more collegial forms of leadership and servanthood; and

5. consideration of new models of congregational life and witness.

Yearly Themes:

The following themes are proposed for the years 1995–2000. Each theme is focused on ministry with Christ. It is envisioned that themes will be used in three-year cycles for the next few years. This will allow program developers and worship planners to benefit from the large number of resources available for use with the Revised Common Lectionary. Throughout these three-year cycles it will not be necessary for weekly themes to focus so tightly on the annual theme that their relationship to the Christian calendar is obscured. Annual themes should be more illustrative than definitive as weekly themes are developed. With these ideas in mind, the following are suggested as annual themes for the years 1995–2000:

1995: "Discovering the Christ"

Life is a continual process of risk, growth, evaluation, planning, and further risk. The life and ministry of Christ are the examples of one who grasped a vision and risked all for its fulfillment. Congregations that hope to experience joy in their ministries will seek to discover where and how Jesus is at work around and among them. They will look for Christ in their community, among their people, and within themselves. Such congregations must honestly reflect on their past, engage in constructive ministries in the present, and strive to be active participants with God in creating the future together. The theme for 1995 focuses on the call to "Discover the Christ" through personal and congregational assessment to discern their unique calling, and then join Christ in moving into the future with joy and hope.

1996: *"Journeying with Christ"*

Personal spiritual growth is an important concern in the contemporary world. Today many people are asking foundational life questions relating to their personal journey and how that journey relates to the witness and message of the church. The church is a body of individuals who are also striving to be faithful to the call to "Journey with Christ" in the midst of an increasingly complex world. The 1996 theme focuses on questions of personal meaning and the relationship between one's personal journey, one's journey with others, and the call of Christ to be disciples and witnesses.

1997: *"Living Together in Christ"*

The church is called to be the living body of Christ in the world. As such the disciples of Jesus are challenged to live a life of integrity, mutuality, intentional harmony, and acceptance of others. Discovering what it means to be the family of God is a primary motivation for all Christians. With equal regard for others, each individual is called to live in full partnership with people of other cultures, races, and faith movements. Congregations that hope to express joy must be groups of people who know how to "in honor prefer one another." The 1997 theme calls the church to bear witness that God loves and accepts each person by "Living Together in Christ."

1998: "Transforming Communities with Christ"

The faith community is built on the call to "seek to bring forth and establish the cause of Zion." In contemporary terms this is the call to transform our local and global communities into places where justice and equal regard for all are primary values. Such a call is more than a desire to do community service. It unites us with others as we look at how our church communities (congregations) and our physical communities can be transformed by the indwelling power of the Holy Spirit. It is also a call that causes us to be involved in many of life's arenas, including the educational, economic, and political. In 1998 the call to be "Transforming Communities with Christ" is rich with symbolism and can offer a fresh look at the witness of Zion-building.

1999: "Serving Joyfully in Christ"

Servant ministry is exemplified in the way Jesus washed the feet of his disciples. In the contemporary world the witness of servant ministry is desperately needed and will cause disciples to recognize the need to give compassionate, competent, and courageous ministry. We enter into witness and service by our recognition that divine Grace has touched us and freed us of guilt and fear. The positive witness of "Serving Joyfully in Christ" will be important in 1999 as the Saints face the inevitable apocalyptic themes that will be so much a part of the culture in that year.

2000: "Enriching Life Through Christ"

In the process of witnessing, it is important for the church and for individual Saints to stand for responsible, sustainable care of the earth, its people, and its resources. All those who are disciples of Christ are called to explore the nature of abundant life, not just for self, but for all of God's children. The 1998 theme offers the opportunity for the church to lift up the importance of witnessing through our actions as well as our words. The affirmation of "Enriching Life Through Christ" offers hope for an abundant life as we honor all of life as a sacred creation of God.

Use of Themes in Worship and Programming

The congregations of the church utilize themes in two primary ways. First, they use the weekly themes as the basis for worship planning. Second, congregational leaders use the annual theme as a central focus around which to plan special events, pastoral care activities, and educational activities.

With these considerations in mind, the church will no longer publish monthly themes. These themes do not appear to have a strong purpose and they make it necessary for theme developers to harmonize the four (or five) weekly themes in a month in an artificial way. This is particularly true as Easter moves from month to month. Without the necessity of developing monthly themes, weekly themes can be more closely linked to appropriate seasons of the Christian calendar, and worship and program planners can take greater advantage of materials that are widely available in the greater Christian community such as the Revised Common Lectionary materials.

Instead of monthly themes, a set of monthly program focuses are being suggested to the field. Thus at the intersection of the annual theme and each monthly program focus, it will be possible to develop weekly themes that will be usable in worship as well as other areas of church life.

Leonard M. Young

CHAPTER 15

A Concluding Word

The significance of the Aaronic priesthood cannot be overemphasized. Nor can members of the Aaronic quorum forget the call for responsible and personal service. The Aaronic priesthood as a presence, and being present, are in the best position to respond.

But I would draw your attention to one final responsibility—the need to take care of yourselves and of each other. Long years of dedicated service take a toll. People need to *receive* as well as give. If there is a fault that might be identified among our concerned priesthood, it is the fault of overextension.

It is important to remember the price of dedicated service, and be willing to acknowledge, support, reach out, and care for others who, like yourself, are giving of themselves. Lift up the priesthood in your prayers and in your concerns, and, by the same token, be sure that others are aware of your needs so that they might be of help.

It is a wonderful and fearsome task to be Christ's hands and feet in a wounded world.

Paul M. Edwards

APPENDIX

The Mentor/Ordinand Concept

In the experience of the church, there are times when forms of mentoring should be focused on the support of those who are assuming specific new roles or tasks. For these situations, there are other mentoring forms that may be helpful. Mentoring of vocational roles in secular life is of growing interest in many businesses and institutions. Also, mentoring for church institutional roles in specific priesthood offices or congregational responsibilities is encouraged in some stakes and regions.

The following mentor/ordinand concept is one model for such a relationship that may be used to establish the kind of mutually supportive relationship to help a disciple move into a new avenue of service and witness.

Definitions

The **mentor** is one who has served or is serving in the priesthood office to which the ordinand is called and may best be understood as a tutor, guide, coach, friend, example, corroborator, and supporter.

The **ordinand** is one who has been called to a priesthood office, but who has not yet been ordained or may have been ordained recently and may best be understood as a learner, trainee, follower, and associate.

Relationships

The mentor/ordinand relationship is primarily one of two friends and co-workers. It suggests the yoking of an experienced priesthood member with a less experienced one in regard to the office to which the ordinand has been called, as exemplified by the Paul/Timothy relationship in the New Testament.

The mentor/ordinand relationship is committed solely to the success of the apprentice.

Mentor/ordinand relationships will be diverse and varying according to the nature of the two persons who constitute the relationship.

Role of the Mentor

The role of the mentor is to provide assistance to the ordinand and his or her family in the form of counsel, orientation, initial training, and continuing support in regard to the new responsibility being assumed.

Each mentor is challenged to prayerfully consider the critical nature of his or her role in the development of the ordinand. The success of the process will be directly related to the perceived significance of it.

The mentor will want to have the ordinand participate with him or her in all aspects of the new responsibility, with the exception of the administration of the ordinances of the church. These ordinances, however, should be fully discussed and observed. This will help facilitate the ordinand's adjustment to new leadership roles and tasks.

The mentor will serve for a period approximating one year. This time frame is variable depending on the needs of the ordinand. It may sometimes even be necessary for the ordinand to have a different mentor as time passes. The mentor should focus on the following:

- participating in the ordination service of the new priesthood member;
- encouraging and helping in the enrollment of the ordinand in orientation studies and experiences which may be appropriate;

- acting as a resource person to familiarize the ordinand with current policies, procedures, programs, and resources relating to the new area of responsibility;
- assisting in providing a support group for the enrichment of the ordinand and his or her family;
- assisting the ordinand in adjusting to new assignments in connection with the newly assumed responsibility; and
- helping to sensitize the ordinand's supervisor to the needs of the ordinand.

Role of the Ordinand

The role of the ordinand is to receive and respond to the assistance offered by the mentor. This is not merely a passive role, however. The ordinand needs to probe for and request the kinds of help that will enable him or her to acquire the insights and skills needed to become reasonably proficient in the new area of responsibility.

Each ordinand is challenged to prayerfully consider the critical nature of his or her role in the mentoring process. Its success will be directly related to the perceived significance of it.

Program

The mentor/ordinand program is intended to identify the areas of help to be provided to and with the ordinand in order for him or her to become motivated toward providing effective leadership to and with others. It is envisioned to include four need areas: personal and family, orientation, continuing support, and evaluation.

Personal and Family. Before ordination the ordinand and his or her family may benefit from a personal discussion centered on the sharing of feelings about the new responsibility. This discussion should include the mentor, the ordinand, and as many family members as possible. This opportunity to share feelings may enhance their personal sense of belonging and colleagueship. It will also serve to defuse fears about the new role of responsibility, help the ordinand and his or her family to begin to feel comfortable with it, and provide an opportunity to state initial questions and concerns verbally.

Orientation. Shortly after the call is accepted, the ordinand should be contacted by the mentor or supervisor to discuss more specifically their new responsibility. The ordinand should be provided with whatever position definitions, job descriptions, and principle responsibilities pertain to this new role and whatever other resources, study materials, guidelines, and articles might be appropriate. Some discussion pertaining to

- the larger, more comprehensive goal framework in which the ordinand will be working;
- other leaders on the total team of workers to whom he or she will be relating; and
- the more comprehensive study program to enrich his or her ministry—perhaps involving Temple School; professionally sponsored institutes, workshops, and seminars; reading bibliographies appropriate to continuing development of the ordinand; and perhaps other matters would certainly be in order.

It is during this session that the channels of communication are opened and the spirit of cooperation is established.

Continuing Support. Faithful follow-through must be initiated by the mentor and expected of the ordinand with regard to regular meetings together concerning the study or practical assignments made from time to time. Encouragement needs to be provided to the ordinand in all of this to maintain and develop personal gifts, abilities, and skills in relation to performing the assigned tasks.

Fitting into a "pigeonhole" or imitating a stereotyped impression of role or task performance is to be avoided.

Evaluation. Near the end of the mentoring period, review and evaluation procedures should be brought into play. This must be comprehensive in nature and should be an exercise in complete candor by the mentor and ordinand in preparation for the formal termination of the assigned relationship between them and the continuing development of the ordinand on his or her own. Specific position definitions, job descriptions, principal responsibilities, and the ordinand's feelings and performance in relationship to them will be an important part of the evaluation process. No negative judgments should be offered by the mentor in this process—only positive reinforcement, affirming suggestions for the future, and expressions of continuing support. The pastor of the ordinand's congregation should conduct a formal priesthood review at the end of the first year after the ordination.

Guidelines for Getting Started

The initial meeting between the mentor and the ordinand should be conducted soon after acceptance of the priesthood call. At this meeting, the mentor should do the following:

- Arrange for an informal visit with the family.
- Encourage the ordinand to enroll in appropriate pre-ordination Temple School classes.
- Agree on a timetable for regular personal meetings on at least a monthly basis.
- Review your schedules for the next year and determine if there will be activities the mentor and the ordinand might share together in ministry (such as workshops and seminars, preaching series, reunions, and youth camps).

- Finalize a "covenant" between the mentor and ordinand. In effect, this covenant is an agreement to be available for fellowship, counseling, and just being a friend. It would be helpful to include items such as a specific time for prayer support and a time for regular contacts by phone or letter.

After this meeting the pastor should be given an opportunity to review the arrangements made between the ordinand and the mentor. This will keep the pastor informed and offer an opportunity for input into the mentoring process which may prove helpful to the ordinand in future ministry. The mentor should take the initiative to check with the pastor concerning possible meetings and times for mutual ministries, as outlined above.

Selection of Mentors

The careful selection of a mentor for an ordinand will be essential to the success of the mentor-ordinand concept. The following criteria should be considered indicative of those who could serve as good mentors. A mentor should have

- an exciting sense of mission and positive discipleship;
- a willingness to share in a mutual learning environment;
- a willingness to share in discovering and releasing giftedness;
- a commitment to the principle of continuing personal growth and development;
- a nonjudgmental disposition that enables affirmation and patient encouragement of the ordinand;
- an established collegial relationship with the ordinand;
- a reasonably compatible "wavelength" of understanding with the ordinand;

- a reasonably close geographical proximity to the ordinand; and
- an attitude supportive of World Church and regional/stake officers and programs.

Leonard M. Young
John T. Conway

- Excerpted from *Congregational Leaders Handbook* (Herald House, 1994), *Christian Mentoring: "Two Models"*, Vision, B–2.

BIBLIOGRAPHY

I. Temple School Courses to Aid Aaronic Skills

General

PA101   **The Deacon**

PA102   **The Teacher**

PA103   **The Priest**

Office-centered courses open to all students. Priesthood members will more clearly understand roles and functions and improve skills for more effective ministry. Others will develop an understanding and appreciation of the importance of priesthood ministry to congregational life.

CL100   **Ministry with Persons.** Explores the nature of pastoral care and how members of the congregation may become engaged in caring ministry to one another. (1991)

CL101   **Introduction to Pastoral Care.** An overview of concepts concerning caring ministries in the congregation. (1989)

CL105   **Family Ministry.** Explores the nature and role of the family in today's society, discusses communication skills for families, and suggests some basic skills for ministering to the special needs of families. (1994)

PA120   **Congregational Life.** Focuses on what it means, theologically and practically, to be a congregation of the church. Examines various organizational alternatives and suggests ways of identifying and implementing a philosophy of ministry. Special emphasis is given to developing and working with commissions in the various areas of congregational life. (1987)

PA121   ***Communication Skills.*** Presents basic concepts and engages students in skill-building exercises designed to increase the effectiveness of communication among leaders and members of the congregation. (1982)

PA260   ***Priesthood Ministry of Women.*** This course is designed to help the learner appreciate the opportunities and problems of women who have accepted priesthood responsibilities. Every person would find this course beneficial to better understand servant ministry within the broadening context of the RLDS priesthood. (1986)

TE210   ***Christian Ethics for Leaders.*** This course deals with how Christians determine what kinds of behaviors are "right" and "good." It is concerned with the process by which we make moral claims or rules, the means by which we determine them, and how we apply them. (1989)

TE230   ***Spiritual Disciplines.*** This course provides insight into the practice of spiritual disciplines and includes units on spirituality and discipline, fasting, prayer, meditation, and living in community. (1993)

AM152   ***Aaronic Ministry Today.*** This course examines the nature of the Aaronic priesthood as a unique and essential ministry in the modern world. Material draws on *Guidelines for Priesthood,* which calls for concentration on priesthood as a servant ministry role. Explores the nature of authority as meeting genuine need compassionately. Traces origins and how priesthood members are related to one another, to others who minister, and to others who receive ministry. Poses options for pursing excellence through faith, study, increased competence, and wide practical application. (1991)

Peace Issues and Conflict Resolution

TL101   ***The Temple: Ensign of Peace.*** Explores a variety of ways that the Temple can promote the cause of peace. Authors from around the world, inside and outside the church, have shared their thoughts and feelings on how the church can promote peace through the ministries of the Temple. (1990)

TL103   ***Abundant Life and the Temple.*** The Temple Abundant Life Center models ministries for inner peace, reconciliation in primary relationships, and wholeness of body, mind, and spirit. This course explores the search for abundant life, the faith journey, wholeness through suffering, questions of identity, and ministries of the Temple that can enhance an abundant life. (1992)

AM133   ***Church Peacemaker Skills.*** Deals with the concept of "watchcare." The peacemaker promotes unity and ministers toward reconciliation in the body of Christ. Topics include standards for helping others; unity and group stresses; listening; conflict and personal stresses; asserting, resolving, and reconciling; iniquity and serious offenses; privacy and real helping events; and repentance and forgiveness. (1992)

CL202   ***Conflict Management in the Church.*** This course discusses causes of interpersonal and group conflict characteristic of congregational life. Practical methods of defining and effectively coping with such conflict are presented. (1989)

PS220   ***Personal Peace and Community.*** This course presents peace in relation to the Prince of Peace, Jesus Christ. People are encouraged first to sharpen their own spiritual tools and then live out the gospel through community action on behalf of the world. (1994)

Counseling and Interpersonal Ministry

PA300B ***Interpersonal Ministry: Counseling Skills.*** Presents the skills and techniques of counseling as applied in church leadership roles. Both theory and practical application exercises are provided. (1983)

PS210 ***With Equal Regard.*** This course explores how we view each other and how we respond to differences between us. Mutuality is examined in relation to models, issues, language, power, and change. (1992)

CL275 ***Cultural and Ethnic Sensitivity.*** Deals primarily with planting congregations cross-culturally. Attention is given to evaluating the strengths and weaknesses of various models of ministry. Additional emphasis is given to overcoming common cultural and personal interaction problems. (1988)

PS212 ***Working for Life: Dismantling Racism.*** A Christian-based resource using experiential exercises under the headings of awareness, education, advocacy, and activism. This course seeks to move the participant from personal insight toward a lifetime commitment of growth, accountability, and service in reconciliation and peace in human relationships. (1992)

PA330 ***Ministry to the Dying and Bereaved.*** This course can help individuals recognize personal beliefs about death and dying, identify the bereavement process, explore how children react to death, evaluate legal and financial issues related to death, and discuss ways individuals and congregations can assist in grief ministry. (1994)

II. Resources from Herald House

Journey of Forgiveness by Barbara Howard

Reconciliation and healing relationships are needed in the church today. This study course is designed to enable people to develop skills in forgiving. The seven-session course contains stated objectives as well as individual and class activities. The territory of "disabling nonforgiveness" is explored as are the creative possibilities in forgiveness as personal and political activity.

Journey of Joy by Barbara Howard

The Christian experience is meant to be a journey of joy. In this insightful, seven-session study course suitable for individual or small-group use, Barbara Howard begins the journey at home—within the human spirit. Through numerous stories, examples, meditations, and activities she takes the pathways of love, courage, celebration, and peace. The true importance of this journey is not so much in arriving but in letting go and journeying together.

The Witness of Reconciliation by Wallace B. Smith

These six lectures on reconciling ministry were presented by President Wallace B. Smith to members of the Central Field in September and October 1991. President Smith addresses reconciliation with our history as a religious movement, with God, with each other, within the body of Christ, in the world community, and with all of God's creation.

The Promise of Healing by Geoffrey Spencer

In six lectures, Apostle Spencer discusses the following topics:
- The Search for Healing
- The Reality of Healing
- Where Is God When...?
- What Kind of World?
- The Compassionate God
- The Church as Healing Agent

***Committed to Peace* by Barbara Higdon**
This series of talks given at the Temple in fall 1993 addresses "Visions of a Peaceable Kingdom," "A Global Family," and "The Roots of Violence."

***Worship in a Diverse Culture* by Peter Judd**
A series of lectures on the nature of worship, delivered by the director of the Temple Worship Center at the Temple in 1994.

***Congregation Missionary System* compiled by Alex Kahtava, Sr.**
Provides guidance for pastoral unit leaders in providing for effective missionary outreach. Revised and updated in 1995 for inclusion in *Congregational Leaders Handbook* (*A Witnessing Community: The Congregation Missionary System*, Mission, C–4).

***The Priesthood Manual* (1990)**
The latest edition of this very informative and significant manual.

III. Adult Texts for Reunion

***Discovering the Christ* (1995) by Donald Breckon**
This reunion text takes a refreshing look at the ministry of Jesus. Breckon encourages the reader to examine and re-examine the questions Jesus asked the people, rather than the answers that have survived through time and translation. Perhaps the timeless questions he asked are of more value to think about years later than the time and culturally bound answers that were recorded.

Too often people expend their energies arguing about the *correct* responses and not enough time developing a personal response to these life-sustaining questions. Each day the class will study material to help them develop their own response to these questions: "Who do you say that I am?", "Why do you ignore the log in your own eye?", "What is the first and greatest commandment of them all?", "Why should God reward you if you love only the people who love you?", "Why stand ye here all the day idle?"

The Gift of Peace (1994) by Carolyn and David Brock

This adult reunion text provides a wealth of material to help individuals, congregations, and interest groups expand their understanding of peace issues. The authors have provided a wide variety of readings, exercises, and learning experiences to help people explore peace in many arenas of life. Among the topics explored are the concept of Jesus as a peacemaker, the opportunities for congregations to practice the presence of peace, the congregation as educator for peace, and outreach possibilities in the local community as well as in the larger human community.

Living the Gospel in Our Many Worlds (1988) by Richard and Barbara Howard

This text is a study course that moves the reader through the worlds of self, family, friendship, neighbor, nation, and planet. As the concerns of each world expand, so does the call to care and witness.

Each class session offers several activities and discussion questions, and the material is adaptable to small or large groups.

The final sessions explore the church's larger mission in the world and the First Presidency's emphasis on ministries of peace and reconciliation related to the Temple and priesthood development.

Blessed Are the Peacemakers (1990) by Elbert A. Dempsey, Jr.

This text examines the theological and practical basis of peace. To the author peacemaking involves recognizing the legitimacy of other people's perspectives and allowing them to grow, to make their contributions, to experience what the ancient Hebrews called *shalom*, which denotes peace, whole-

ness, and healing. Using scriptural background and modern research, Dempsey provides a practical way to analyze conflicts and apply appropriate conflict management techniques to problems commonly encountered in congregational, family, and personal life.

A Time for Healing (1991) by Shirley VanRiette

A prophetic church challenges its people to rise and courageously move out with God in offering healing ministry to a hurting world. As servants of Jesus Christ, it is our responsibility to reach out and share God's redeeming love.

Through scriptures, personal testimonies, activities, and class discussion, this course encourages readers to explore ways that love can bring healing to ourselves, our families, our congregations, and our communities, giving them new life and hope for the future.

IV. General Resources

Fowler, J. W. *Weaving the New Creation*. San Francisco: HarperCollins Publishers, 1991.

Martin, Mike W. *Everyday Morality: An Introduction to Applied Ethics*. Belmont, California: Wadsworth Publishing Company, 1995.

Mead, L. B. *The Once and Future Church: Reinventing the Congregation to a New Mission Frontier*. Washington, D.C.: The Alban Institute, 1991.

Nouwen, Henri J. M. *The Return of the Prodigal Son*. New York: Doubleday, 1992.

Sample, Tex. *U.S. Lifestyles and Mainline Churches*. Louisville, Kentucky: Westminster/John Knox Press, 1990.

Soelle, Dorothee and Shirley A. Cloyes. *To Work and To Love*. Philadelphia: Fortress Press, 1988.